# Shiny

## How to Stop Being a Social Media Magpie

# Karen Skidmore

# Shiny Shiny

## How to Stop Being a Social Media Magpie

ISBN 978-1-849-14255-7

First Edition 2012
First published in Great Britain 2012

## www.ShinyShinyBook.com

To my dad, who would have been tickled pink to have my book on his bookcase

# CONTENTS

# FOREWORD

Magpies are curious and intriguing birds. They share with us humans a degree of self-awareness. For example, they can recognise their own reflection in a mirror. They are also compulsive collectors and their keen eyes are readily drawn to shiny objects. Like some humans too, their actions are somewhat autonomic and fruitless, as the things they collect mainly have no intrinsic value.

Some social media so-called gurus flit like a magpie from one shiny new platform to another with no more of a strategy than a desire to collect vast numbers of followers. Their motivation is to merely fluff up their online plumage and ego. In this world however quality always wins over quantity. With a plethora of social media platforms available, a workable strategy will always win over a scattergun approach.

I've been fortunate to know Karen for several years now. Even more fortunately, she has a serendipitous habit of turning up in my life just about when I am about to augment or reinvent my online presence.

What's so good about this is the time I save by listening to her advice and following her lead. Karen has an uncanny knack of having her finger on the pulse and she dispenses no nonsense practical advice rather than theory. She knows how to build an online nest that will not only last for years but also be readily extensible.

If you are a fledgling in the world of social media, Shiny Shiny, is the book for you. If you have been active in the social media world for some time but your eggs have yet to hatch, Shiny Shiny is also the book for you.

If you are interested in using social media to grow your business what you need right now is not same-old, same-old but a high level, yet simple, approach that works.

The advice dispensed in this book will save you from hours, days and weeks of frustration. Follow it and you will learn how to make shiny objects of real value that will have clients flocking around your nest and admiring its build quality.

**Tom Evans**
**Author of Flavours of Thought and**
**Architect of Recipes for Fresh Thinking**

# ARE YOU A SOCIAL MEDIA MAGPIE?

Rebecca is a coach. She wants to help women who have experienced bad relationship breakdowns. She's got a basic website together, printed some business cards and leaflets but she hasn't a clue where to start finding her new clients.

She's been along to a local networking event and met an approachable chap called Simon. Simon runs a coaching business too and is proudly tweeting and updating his Facebook profile at regular intervals during the meeting. Rebecca has heard of Twitter and Facebook. Both seem to be in the newspaper headlines most weeks because of some footballer or Big Brother star that have got themselves in trouble with a tweet or two.

But she's not really understood why anyone would use them in their business. Simon is full of enthusiasm. He tells her that he spends most of his day tweeting, commenting and liking and proudly explains that he's up to 5,412 Twitter followers and it won't be long before he has reached his maximum on Facebook Friends.

Simon is "talking" to people all over the world and he's always on the lookout for the latest app that will help him reach out to more people. His Klout score is up, he's listed on all the Twitter directories and regularly checks (and tweets) his influencer ratings on any website he can find that shows it.

Rebecca is impressed and is very excited to get back to her office to sign up to all the websites Simon has recommended.

She spends the next couple of weeks getting stuck in and creating her new accounts. She begins to realise that what seems simple to start is beginning to get more and more complicated. Rebecca decides she needs to learn as much as possible about this new social media world and reads every blog she can find.

She starts signing up for all the dozens and dozens of free webinars and teleseminars that promise to show her the "quickest and fastest way to make money on social media". She's trying out a couple of websites that promise to give her 10,000 new followers in the next month ... all automatically, without her having to do a thing except grant access to her account.

She begins downloading apps on to her phone to help manage her social media accounts so she can keep up with it all, even when she's away from her desk. And she loves having an email come through alerting her to every new follower – after all, it's only polite to check them out, reply to them and try to start a conversation every time.

Rebecca is beginning to feel like she knows what she is doing. She's loving all this social media stuff and spends hours on it every day. She's able to give other people advice on how to set up their profiles and has even written a few articles for her blog on how best to use social media to grow a new business.

But wait!

Wasn't Rebecca a coach? A coach who wanted to focus on helping women who had experienced a relationship breakdown?

What has "how to use social media to grow your business" articles got to do with dealing with emotional rejection?

Why would you be impressed with social media influencer scores when all you care about is how to mend your breaking heart?

The reality is that Rebecca may have a few thousand Twitter followers, be chatting to friends on Facebook all over the world and have got herself a 87% influencing rank according to one website, but her bank balance is looking rather small.

All this focus on the latest social media sites and the applications that are designed to improve your effectiveness and efficiency in building a business has only resulted in Rebecca feeling very, very poor.

Yes, a few clients have called up and arranged some one-to-one sessions. But these few clients are not going to allow Rebecca to feel her business could support her, let alone her family and partner's expectations for her to contribute to the household budget.

Unfortunately, Rebecca has become victim of the virus that is infecting today's entrepreneurs and small business owners all around the world...

　... The Magpie Syndrome

## Why magpies?

Magpies are notorious birds for swooping down and collecting stuff that glitters in the sun. When they bring it back to their nest, most of it is not wanted. Milk bottle tops, silver foil, lost keys – they don't help make the nests or feed their chicks.

They are intelligent birds. They are even reported to recognise themselves in their reflection, a trait rarely found outside humankind.

But, even though these shiny objects are worthless and pointless to their existence, they still catch their eye and feel compelled to bring them home.

Having helped thousands of coaches, trainers and consultants with their marketing plans and strategies over the past eight years, I see the same thing happen over web tech marketing tools, in particular social media sites such as Twitter and Facebook.

Rebecca is not a one-off example. She is, unfortunately, one of many all over the globe.

"I want to set up Facebook, Twitter and LinkedIn this week. Can you help me?"

It's a question I get asked time and time again. My answer? "No"

Setting up these accounts is relatively straightforward. They are free and it usually only takes a few minutes. All you need is to add your name, upload a photo and fill in the forms before you finally click that "save and publish" button.

I promise you, most of it is no more difficult than filling in an online survey.

But getting social media tools to work for your business is an entirely different matter. Once you've set up your profiles, you have to keep them updated, you've got to start engaging and you've got to be clear about the results you are expecting from using these tools.

It's not like becoming part of a directory that potential clients are searching for you on every day (*although, get your profiles set up with the right key word phrases and carefully constructed introductions, it can work that way once you know what you are doing.*)

Social media presents tools that can be highly effective in building a profitable business but most business owners are using them as toys, at best, blindly expecting new clients to be dropping into their laps.

### Symptoms of the Magpie Syndrome

If you are wondering whether you, too, may have the Magpie Syndrome, then check through these symptoms. Do you have any (or all) of these?

### Symptom Number One: unproductive busy-ness

It's easy to get sucked in (and addicted?) and spend hours tweeting, liking and adding comments and replies. Being on Twitter live for hours every day will just NOT work. Not only will it focus your efforts on just one marketing tool (which is dangerous to do especially if Twitter decides to shut down your account one day ... and believe me, that is a reality and could happen to you) it takes your focus away from stuff that could work for you quicker and more effectively with the time that you've got.

You know who you are. You've got Twitter running in the background of your PC so you can jump in every 15 minutes whilst you write that report for your client. You've even got those little alerts going off, giving you a ping every time a new Tweet comes through. You wouldn't want to miss anything, would you?

If you've got your Outlook, or whatever email account you use, open along with your Twitter feed and your Facebook chat switched on ... just in case ... your focus and attention to what really matters in your business is just not going to be there.

You will never have the brain power or mental stamina to create the products that will make you money. You won't be able to find the time to create the programs that will allow you to work with more clients and increased your earnings potential each month.

Social media does work; done in the right way with the right online marketing systems in place, it will attract new clients to your business. But not when done like this kind of unproductive busy-ness, addictive tweeting, liking and commenting will destroy your business.

## Symptom Number Two: Abandoned online profiles

Even worse than the addictive time-suck, is the abandoned profiles scattered over the web. This is a typical characteristic of a social media magpie. They read an article or watch a video and decide to set up a profile on the latest recommended network.

They've got profiles set up on Twitter, Facebook, LinkedIn, Squidoo, Klout, Foursquare, Google+, Stumbleupon, flickr, Xing, YouTube, Vimeo … in fact, you name it, they've got it set up. The more links to your website and the more online profiles, the better – right?

Wrong! Oh, so wrong. The problem with setting up online profiles left, right and centre and then not doing anything with them, is that when someone actually does find you, it will probably be out of date and dust-balled.

You just don't have time to keep updating your profiles and adding status updates that are meaningful to anyone. If you do try to automate the whole updating process, you will, at best, look like an automated spammer.

It's great that you are taking action, but without some thinking, planning and working out how all these online profiles are going to integrate into your overall marketing systems, they aren't really going to substantially grow your business.

If you went to a website's events page, only to find that the latest event listed happened over 18 months ago, you aren't going to think too favourably of this business, are you? Don't they care about their website? Have they given up and closed up shop?

And it's the same with your forgotten, dust balled profiles.

You may not think that anyone is finding your profiles. But just take a moment right now and Google your name. How many online profiles come up when you search for yourself?

You may be pleasantly surprised how visible you are, but click through to any of your profiles and see whether they represent who you are today.

### Symptom Number Three: Business owner turned social media expert

Going back to Rebecca, remember how she started to get more and more obsessed about learning more about social media?

It's easily done. If you like technology, sleep with your smart phone and crave the latest gadget being launched, then I can see you being drawn to all the shiny social media stuff very, very easily.

It's important to take the time to learn and discover the new ways of marketing. You are the one, after all, who cares about your business so it must be you that has to take responsibility to market yourself in the best possible way. The wonderful thing about the internet is the enormous amount of information out there, just waiting for you to access.

But this same wonderful internet, full of information, also has the potential of being the biggest weight around your neck, dragging you down to the depths of information overload.

8

Not so long ago, I had a very enthusiastic business owner on an online training session. He owned a bed and breakfast in the Lake District and was actually already doing quite well with his Facebook Business Page. One recommendation he took from my training session was the importance of creating a landing page that led to someone taking action, preferably signing up and joining his database.

After several email conversations, this guy went off and set up his own landing page. It looked great. But what puzzled me was that he then went on to write a very detailed article on his bed and breakfast blog about how to go and do this for your own Facebook Page.

Why would a potential guest who was looking for a perfect place to rest their weary head during a walking holiday want to know how to create your own Facebook landing page?

Don't turn yourself into a social media expert for your clients … unless, of course, this is your business focus and you intend to make your money this way.

# TOO MUCH CHOICE IS BAD FOR YOU

Too much choice is bad for your business. It's bad for your stress levels. And it's bad for your bank balance.

Do you remember going to a Harvester restaurant in the 80's? My parents used to take my two brothers and me to eat there from time to time. It was the best value for money to feed us all, whilst my dad could have a reasonable bottle of red wine. But the downside was the ordering. It just went on and on and on.

"Would you like chips or potatoes with that?"

"Chips"

"French fries, fat or ripples?"

"Ripples"

"Paprika, spicy or plain?"

"Plain"

"Would you like salad or vegetables?"

… and you can remember the rest, I'm sure.

Thank goodness we were just a family of five. If I had any more brothers or sisters it could have been last orders at the bar before our waitress finished with us.

Too much choice is bad for us. And that's the problem with marketing a business today.

"Would you like to set up a Facebook, Twitter, LinkedIn or YouTube account?"

"Facebook"

"Would that be a personal profile, business page, community page or group?"

"Business page"

"Would you like a landing page, opt-in offer, custom profile image or info page with maximised SEO?"

"Ummmmmmm......"

The choice available to you is massive. It's huge. You've got endless opportunities to market yourself online and most of it doesn't need to cost you a penny.


**Welcome the new shiny world of marketing**

I like to think I was lucky when I first began working for myself. I started up in business in September 2004, the day my eldest daughter started school.

I was eleven years with the same company, starting off as a recruitment consultant selling temps and CVs to HR Managers and Finance Directors and grew quickly through the ranks to become the youngest Regional Director managing 4 branches and 30 staff at the tender age of 27. After two children in my 30's, coming back after my second maternity leave was hard.

I didn't want to do corporate life any more. I hated the politics and I wanted a more flexible career so that when my children started school, I could have the school holidays at home with them.

I trained as a life coach in 2003 – back in the days when people asked me whether I was bothered about having to wear a swimming costume for my new Life Saving career! I had big dreams of earning the equivalent of my corporate income within 12 months of starting up.

After 5 months I had almost given up. I had a website but few clients and very little in the way of any income.

But once I realised that I was a business owner and not a life coach, my whole attitude to marketing myself changed. Back in 2005, blogs where just starting to become popular. Email newsletters had been around for a while but very few businesses where using them to build a mailing list.

I believe I was lucky because I was able to embrace each of the new shiny marketing tools one at a time. I started with email marketing and autoresponders. Blogging began in the autumn of 2005 with my Kick-Ass Marketing Blog; got a few too many strange Google queries coming through from that tag line so left that domain name behind.

I ignored Twitter to start with, thinking it was a waste of time and a fad that would quickly go the way of Friends Reunited. But bit by bit, I embraced the new shiny world of marketing and all that social media had to offer.

By spending the time and energy creating robust online marketing systems, I have been able to create a business that allows me to work when I want. I work whilst my children are at school and kick-back when the school holidays come by. Flexibility and creating time to spend how I want, whilst still earn a good income is my driving force.

I like having a lifestyle business, especially a profitable one.

But I was able to "do" one web tech marketing tool at a time. There was no rush or panic to get a Facebook Page, YouTube TV Channel, LinkedIn profile and Twitter account set up before the weekend. I could dabble, play around and fiddle about without any pressure of keeping up with the Joneses'.

And here lies the big problems you are faced with: too much choice and too much pressure to get it all done RIGHT NOW! You can't read an article about social media without being bashed over the head with "if you don't take action, then you will get left behind" attitude.

It's easy to throw yourself into a blind panic, fly around like a crazed magpie and bring every new shiny tool that is suggested to you back to your nest.

With each new account or web tech tool, it doesn't make a difference to your bottom line. All it seems to do is create another time-suck.

And this is what this book is all about. It's here to help you stop being that social media magpie, stop wasting your time on stuff that doesn't work and focus your energy and resources on creating web tech marketing systems that will work for you … today, tomorrow, when you are holiday, when you are flat out working on client projects and when you want to kick-back and take every Friday off to spend how you want.

Online tools are immensely powerful. And without being online you are going to strangle your business – in today's marketplace you have to be on the web to become profitable and grow.

But there are certain steps to take if you want your online marketing to work for you. And these steps are outlined in this book. Follow them and you will guarantee yourself a profitable business that will enable you to work smarter and give you the choice of how you spend more of your time.

I am fed up with seeing business owners panic when they got told they simply have to be on Facebook and Twitter to be successful.
Advertising agencies, marketing departments, web masters – they all seem to be bolting on "Like Me" Facebook buttons and "Follow Me on Twitter" links to websites and leaflets.

There are too many social media "Gurus" around spouting statistics like bullets from my 10 year old's automatic Nerf Gun. People are being friended on Facebook by national carpet companies and major coffee chains. And I don't know about you, but I don't want to be "friends" with these sorts of brands. And certainly don't consider carpet companies or coffee chains to be on my Christmas card list.

Yes, Facebook is an integral part of our society today. Yes, it has enough members to be considered to be the third biggest country in the world. And yes, you can make money out of having a presence on Facebook.

But being scared into getting a Facebook Business Page without the right marketing tools and systems in place is going to waste your time. You are going to end up a social media magpie with nothing more to show than a nest full of shiny new toys.

So stop flying around looking for the next shiny object that is supposed to rocket your business success over night and start laying down the right foundations to your online marketing.

It's a harder path to follow and will take longer than you imagine ... but it will give you so much more than the short-term make-a-quick-buck approach, that gets you nowhere fast.

### All that glitters is not gold ...

If I wrote this book just three years ago, I would be writing about MySpace and Google Wave. Today our eyes and ears are attracted to social media trends such as hashtags, Google+, Foursquare and Klout scores. And by the time you are reading this book, there will probably be plenty more names to add to the list who claim to be the next hottest tool to be used.

At the time of writing this book, I have to confess that I have not even tried to get my head around Google+. Yes, I've signed up for an account, added my photo and relevant website links but I just haven't had the time to do any more than that.

This may seem a foolish approach to take, especially being a web marketing expert. Shouldn't I, of all people, be in there, making my mark and building my connections?

The problem is that all that glitters is not gold. Yes, I have no doubt that Google+ will evolve and become serious competition for Facebook. The way Google is integrating their social network into their search engine algorithms and pay-per-click ads is very interesting. And I know, at some point, I will have taken the time to work out my Google+ strategy and how to integrate it into the rest of my marketing.

Who knows ... you may be reading this now and be quietly scoffing at my lack of foresight to "get in early."

But, I just want to use this example to prove a point here. Just because a new shiny toy has been presented to the business world, doesn't mean that you have to trip yourself up and rush to sign up for the Beta version because there are only limited invitations available.

Even now that Google+ is open to everyone and anyone, I know that my target audience are still not convinced whether it's the right tool for them to use. They are still too busy getting their heads around Facebook and Twitter.

This will obviously change over the coming months and years, but for now Google+ is not going to make a difference to my profitability in the next couple of months. I have my goals. I know what I am focused on. I am clear on my marketing strategy, what tools I am using and, more importantly, how I am going to use them.

And I am not going to change any of these over night because of some mad rush for the hills, only to discover it's only fools' gold rather than the real thing.

By taking the time to write this book, this is what I want for you.

I want you to have a clear, consistent web tech marketing strategy that evolves over time. There is no need to take knee-jerk decisions, even in this fast paced business world that we have today.

If you have the foundations set down right first, then it's easier and more profitable for you to try out the new shiny toys that are right for you. And, more importantly, for reaching out and engaging with your clients.

**Old school rules**

There is no doubt that how you do business today has changed massively over the past ten years. The internet and smart phone technology have been instrumental in these changes. And it's no surprise that many of you have found the whole change process tough.

I was at school during the 80's and, like so many others from this generation, I didn't have much in the way of IT lessons. I remember the hot room that my class used to go to with 6 or 7 big machines whirling away. We were taught how to write a basic macro program so that the words "my name is Karen" scrolled endlessly up the screen.

I had typing lessons – yup, on electronic typewriters – and when we set about any publishing projects it involved sticky back plastic and scissors (my kind of copy and paste.)

My children are now 10 and 12. They are beginning to know how to search safely on Google to do research for their homework projects, along with the watchful eye of their mum and dad. They go to YouTube to watch their friends' latest videos they've created and added to their TV channel. They log into their school email system from home to access documents and class notes. They have absolutely no problem finding and downloading apps on to my iPhone and Skyping their buddies at the weekend.

It's a different world, isn't it?

And how we do business and communicate with each other has changed. There are new rules to follow and keep up with, whether we like it or not.

Fifteen years ago, the only ways to seek out and attract new clients involved advertising, direct mail and good old fashioned cold-calling. I worked in recruitment back then and although it wasn't any harder or easier, it was a whole lot simpler.

If I wanted to get more temps out working on a Monday morning, I knew what I had to do. I had to get regular letters out the door, I had to follow them up with phone calls, arrange client visits and do it all again the following week.

If I worked in recruitment today, I just know there would be many more things that I would have to do to get the business I wanted. The rules have changed.

Communications have multiplied: email, LinkedIn messaging, commenting on a Facebook update, tweeting, direct messaging, chat room, texting … the list goes on and on. We can't go anywhere without our smart phones that bleep, ring and vibrate with every new notification and message.

Understanding these new rules of communication is important. Just because you have the ability to communicate on so many different levels, doesn't necessarily mean you should. And it certainly doesn't mean that you send out the same message on every different medium.

Have you ever had someone try to call you, leave a message, then text you and also write a quick email to make sure you get the message they want you to get. Overwhelming and annoying, isn't it? You feel you are being bombarded. So imagine how it feels to your potential client when they see the same message with the same, exact words on their Facebook, LinkedIn and Twitter newsfeeds. It's not exactly personal, is it?

The problem with using all these new communication tools and platforms is that it's easy to forget the old school rules: basic marketing principles are being ignored.

Here are the old school rules that seem to get ignored in the new shiny world of marketing.

**People buy from people ... not from avatars**

This is especially so if you are selling "you" –
coaching, training, mentoring, consulting, design,
support. Your clients just won't respond well to an
automated message on their phone from a speed-
dialling call center robot, so why do it with endless
automated tweets on Twitter?

**Too much screen time makes you dull**

You were warned about computer games when you
were younger, weren't you? (And you probably tell
your own kids today.) Too much staring at the
screen is bad for your health, stifles your creativity
and productivity and it certainly doesn't help
develop your real-life social skills.

**Speaking to people works**

See that black, plastic small box on your desk ... the
one with a handset, gathering dust? Yup, that's a
telephone. And as you spend more time staring at
screens and "talking online", I bet that you've
forgotten how to use it.

**Snail mail works, too**

OK, the cost of stamps here in the UK is quite
ridiculous and you probably want to be considering
exactly who you send stuff to in the post and watch
your costs. But the amount of direct mail that lands
on your doormat has reduced significantly over
recent years. The majority of businesses have moved

over to the cheaper communications such as email and social media, but the savvy business owners are still using it.

### Know exactly who you want to attract

Before you do any marketing, whether it's direct mail, email campaign or social media you absolutely, have to, without question ... know your target client. Without this critical foundation step, you will fail. And fail bad.

Make sure you read Step One in this book very carefully if you've forgotten to do this before embarking on your Twitter and Facebook campaigns.

### One pillar of marketing is not going to hold you up

I'm sure you can all conjure up a picture of the Pantheon, the incredible temple in the heart of Rome. If there were just one pillar, or even three or four, the enormous roof and entrance just wouldn't stay up. And it's the same with your marketing.

Rely on social media (and yes, I consider the likes of Twitter, Facebook and LinkedIn to be just one pillar rather than three) as your only means of attracting new clients and you run a very risky marketing strategy. So although this book is focusing on social media as a way of attracting clients, NEVER rely on it. Make sure you are using plenty of other pillars such as speaking, article writing, advertising, networking, referral schemes, joint ventures and so on.

## Your database is king

The problem with creating a following on many of the social networking sites is exactly that. It's all on the social networking site. If that particular social networking decided one day that you weren't sticking to their terms of services and cancelled your account ... you are stuffed, aren't you? And don't go thinking this will never happen, because it does. Even to professional, honest business owners like yourself.

You don't own your social network. It's owned by the website you're using. So it's critical you create a marketing trail that leads your social network to your website and ultimately to subscribe to your database. This is explained in detail in Step Four and Five and if you follow the suggestions I make, it will dramatically increase your results.

# Shiny Shiny Mindset

A big part of creating successful web tech marketing systems is the state of your mindset and attitude towards it all. It's like food shopping on an empty stomach, without a list. You go in for bread and milk and you come out with a basket full of high sugar snacks.

It's the same with social media. Go in hungry for the latest new shiny toy and without a plan or marketing strategy, your nest is going to fill up quickly.

*You will notice little warnings throughout this book. **Magpie Alerts** have been added at certain points, particularly when I make recommendations on certain websites or applications to check out.*

It's really important to me that this book doesn't do the exact opposite of what I set out to do – instead of stopping you be a social media magpie, it turns you into one.

Believe me, I'm not perfect. I've got the "I was a Twitter Addict" T-shirt, along with the "I couldn't sleep without making sure that checking my emails is the last and first thing I do every day" so I know how easy it is to get caught out with faffing about with the tools, rather than focusing your time on planning, acting on those plans and getting your web tech marketing systems so that they create clients for you.

Our smart phones are indeed a technological brilliance. It's like having your office in your back pocket. But they can also kill a marriage, destroy your relationship with your children and make you a very dull person at social and business events.

So look out and pay attention to these **Magpie Alerts**. They are there to stop you flying off to your nest again to surround yourself with all your shiny bounty.

### Completion NOT perfection

This is a mantra that I live and die by, as well as making sure my clients follow as well. You will never, ever finish your website. You will never, ever create a perfect squeeze page. You will never, ever be totally satisfied with that video you've recorded.

Good is good enough and never forget that. It's why you will probably find plenty of typos and grammar errors in this book. Yes, I have had it edited and proof read but I will add to this book from time to time to update and keep up with the fast paced social media world. And I write how I talk.

These **Magpie Alerts** are there to stop you from spending an hour deciding whether your image on a web page looks better 10 pixels to the right or 10 pixels to the left. You haven't time to be faffing about with that stuff.

You're a business owner, not a perfectionist.


## Failed life coach turned business owner

I have another T-shirt stored away in the back of my wardrobe (I like wearing T-shirts.) On the front (in Wham! 80's style font) is emblazoned "Failed Life Coach."

When I first started my own business, I was an accredited life coach. I had big ambitions to build my practice. You know the usual stuff … a six figure business after two years, regular column in Red magazine and an appearance or two on the BBC breakfast sofa.

The problem was that it didn't work out like this. My training to be a life coach covered everything there was to know about coaching. But training me to be a business owner was shoved into a one hour teleclass and a short session in day 2 of the weekend training.

Although I was trained to be a great life coach, it was apparent after five months of going nowhere fast, that I sucked as a business owner.

Things had to change.

You see, I thought of myself as a life coach. I did everything I could do to go out and find clients who wanted to be coached. I think I was on the verge of being reported as a stalker to a couple.

The day I decided to change my way of thinking and become a business owner who happened to offer coaching, was the day things started changing.

I began to take the time to look at the few clients who I was seeing results with and work out why they were coming to me and what it was I doing for them. I began to realise that it wasn't coaching they were buying from me – it was the results and outcomes they were getting. I began to package up my offers – creating programmes and charging more for my time.

And I began to get my head around marketing – building a database, getting known as an expert in my field and creating marketing systems that helped turn strangers into clients.

I stopped calling myself a life coach every time someone asked me what I did and started explaining that I specialised in helping women start up in business (my niche back in 2005).

I began to be a business owner. Now I know not all of you are life coaches. Some of you are trainers, consultants, virtual assistants and designers. But, no matter what profession you are in, all of you are business owners.

Whether you like it or not, you are here to make a profit from your passions, your skills and your knowledge. And the sooner you change your mindset and consider yourself to be a business owner first and foremost, the quicker you will see results. And the quicker you will attract the right clients.

## Avoid the "Do Now"

There are plenty of nuggets and actions for you to take from this book. And I really want you to take action and do the stuff laid out. But it's critical to avoid the "Do Now" attitude that too many of business owners take. As entrepreneurs and business owners, you are naturally creative people. Ideas of new products and names of programs you want to create probably come easily to you.

It's the same with finding new and interesting resources and recommended websites. It's too easy to have a knee-jerk reaction, follow a link and "Do It Now".

I'm all for getting stuff done. Absolutely! And you'll read about how you can make the most of this book and turn ideas in actions next.

But "Do Now" all of your time, and you are going to become a reactive, pin-balling wizard; bouncing around from one website to the next, signing up for this, that and the other. If something recommended to you sounds good, then note it and plan when you are going to do it.

I am sure many of will know Steven Covey's books, especially the 7 Habits of Highly Effective People. It's a classic and a book that I read very early on in my corporate career. The big nugget for me in that book was the way Steven outlined the Time Management Matrix. Sorry to be spouting corporate sounding words at you; I know the words time management and matrix just send shivers down my spine. But the concept works. I've used it for years and it's why I warn you not to get stuck with the "Do Now" attitude.

Steven highlights 4 quadrants: Plan It, Do It, Delegate It and Dump It. Everything you do will fit into one of these quadrants based on whether it's urgent, important or not.

Most of you will be automatically thinking everything is urgent and important and thus deciding you have to "Do It" right there and then. As you start to consciously look at what you are working on throughout the day, you will soon realise that much of what you consider to be "Do It", actually should be in your "Plan It" and even in one of the other two: "Delegate It" and "Dump It".

Next time you are starting your working day, be consciously critical about what you are doing every hour. The more you can move into your "Plan It" quadrant, the more control you will put back in your day. And the more control you have, the quicker and faster you can decide on what needs doing to grow your business.

Stop reacting and doing everything now. Start planning more into your week and you will increase your productivity no end.


### Managing you ... in the time that you have

One thought that is going to pop into your head again and again whist reading this book is wondering how on earth do you find the time to get any of this stuff done. You probably feel as if you are working flat out at the moment (obviously if you are tweeting, liking, commenting and poking all day Ha Ha.)

Therefore, as you read about how to go about setting up your website in the right way, how to set up an autoresponder system and start blogging, I just know you are going have this little shutter come down. "I'm too busy," you will hear yourself whine.

Really? You really feel as if there is not enough time in the day to get all your stuff done?

Pah!

It's not time that's your issue – it's a lack of how you manage yourself in the time that you have.

This may sound harsh ... but it's true. None of us feel that we have enough hours in the day. It's a complaint that slips easily off our tongues. And yet time is one resource that put us all on the same level playing field. We all have 24 hours in the day, 7 days a week.

It's how you choose to spend the hours that you have, that set you apart from your competition.

Yes, yes, yes, some of you are working parents. Having a pre-schooler at home does give you limited work hours – may be even just two half days a week forcing you to burn the midnight candle every evening.

Some of you still have "day-jobs". You are waiting to hand your notice in or accept redundancy terms so if you want a meeting during work hours, it's a juggle to get even just a one day holiday or squeeze it into the weekends.

I'm a mum myself. My children are older now – 10 and 12 – so I work term times and take my foot off the peddle during the school holidays. When I first started up in business in 2004, I was working 3 days a week in a full-on corporate sales environment, racing around with 2 young children doing the nursery runs and all the other mum-jobs that needed doing. Fitting in a new business had to be squeezed in between the hours of 8pm and midnight.

When I handed my notice in and started up on my own, my eldest started school and my youngest was at home with me 2 days a week. I had just 3 short school days to get anything done, plus the obligatory evening shift that kept me up most nights. I had the bumper sticker that said, "Give me one more thing to do and I really will lose the plot."

But when I found myself getting stuck and not moving my new business forward, it wasn't because I didn't have enough time. It was because of two reasons.

Firstly, it was because of a lack of clarity. I didn't have a plan to start with and had no idea what I should be have been doing today, tomorrow and the next. I remember, for example, being so focused on designing my own tri-fold leaflet in my first couple of months that I spent days on it. Honestly, you would have thought I was creating the next piece of art to be hung up in Tate Modern.

These leaflets ended up being chucked in the recycling bin one year later; I had 500 left. They looked terrible and the message was … well, there was no message. Just a whole load of blah, blah. They were really quite crap!

Secondly, it was my lack of self-discipline and how I managed my diary. Being your own boss it great, but without a boss to be accountable to, it's easy to let those things you knew you should be doing, slip on over to the next week.

Over the years I have learnt it pays to schedule appointments in your diary ... with yourself. These appointments aren't moveable and they can't be cancelled. Not for no one, not even a paying client.

The biggest lesson I share with you at how to manage you in the time that you've got is to look closely how you are scheduling appointments in your diary right now.

To start with, take a real hard look at the time you are allowing between appointments. Do you really need an hour to get from one place to another?

Next, are you setting finish times to your meetings and phone calls? Why have two hour meetings when you get the job done in 30 minutes?

Thirdly, take a look at when you are scheduling your appointments. This was a big shift I took last year. For the first seven years of working with clients on a one to one basis via the phone and Skype, I always made my whole day available to my clients. I kept Monday and Friday free for me and my business, but Tuesday, Wednesday and Thursday were available all day from 9am until school pick up.

Then I changed. I realised that I wasn't able to get some big projects moving. My Web Tech Club launch had slipped and slipped and I knew if I didn't make changes to my diary, I would never be able to create and launch other stuff – like this book, for example.

I worked out I was most productive in the morning; straight after school drop off. I told my assistant that clients were now only allowed to schedule sessions from 12noon to 4pm, Monday through to Thursday.

A little voice did creep in and whisper quietly in my ear, "But what if your clients don't like that?" But, do you know what? Not one client has ever objected and I have not had a problem scheduling in a client since.

My most productive time is now serving my business. As my energy starts to wane late morning, my scheduled client calls re-new me and I'm lifted again. So not only do my past, present and future clients benefit from me creating and developing my services and products, but I benefit from my clients giving high energy for the whole day.

I've gone from whining, "I've got no time to get this done" to having 4 mornings a week from 9am to 12noon working on my business. (And yes, I have Fridays to do my own thing, outside of my business, most weeks.)

Try rescheduling your week. Your productivity levels may pleasantly surprise you too.

## Managing your interruptions

This part is going to be short, but sweet.

It you want to increase your productivity, you've got to manage your interruptions.

- Close down your email.

- Switch off all those annoying notifications you've got set that alert you to a new email or tweet.

- Divert your phone or switch it on silent so your answerphone picks up. (I now have my office number on permanent divert, which again has made a massive impact on my productivity. Try it. Do you want to be receptionist as well as MD of your own business?)

- Throw your mobile out of the room. Even if it's set to silent, seeing the screen flash on when a text comes through will distract you.

- Clear your desk. Clutter will only clutter your mind.

- Place a "Do Not Disturb Sign" on your door. If there are other people around you (a partner who works from home or friendly neighbour who likes to stop by for coffee), tell them you do not want to be disturbed whilst you are working.

- If you work from home, turn the washing machine buzzer off (I know you want to hang out the washing before it gets creased but finish what you are doing first.)

- And anything else in and around your working environment that you know distracts you – sort it.

### Managing your ideas and resources

As I've mentioned already, you will find lots of websites, resources and applications recommended throughout this book. And you will also have your own thoughts and ideas that you will collate as you read through each of the steps.

Find a way of keeping track of them all so that you can help yourself to plan action, rather than just knee-jerk your way through. Here are a few ideas on how you manage this.

Scribble in the back of this book. I've left several pages empty for your note taking and idea dumps.

Get yourself a separate notebook to map out your ideas and action plans.

If you prefer online tools (and hey, why wouldn't you if you are reading this book) then a fabulous resource I use daily is Evernote.com. It's a website that allows you collect, store and organize any electronic file, including photos, web links, word docs, PDFs, audio files and so on.

Whatever system works for you set something up to collate your ideas. I don't want you bouncing around from one project to the next because you will find nothing will ever get completed.

For example, if you are currently working on your website (Step Two in this book) and you come up with a cracking idea for a free offer when you read Step Five in this book, then don't stop what you are doing on your website to start your free offer project. Make a note of your free offer idea, decide when you are going to act on it and schedule it in your diary. Finish what you'd planned on doing this week on your website first. Got it? Great.

I'm sharing this with you, from the bottom of my heart, because I've done the "creating lots of ideas & marketing projects all at the same time" juggling act. It just doesn't work.

# KNOWING YOUR WHYS

Before we get stuck into the steps that I have used to create my marketing systems and have helped numerous coaches, trainers and consultants create in their own businesses, it's really important we have a look at your "whys."

Why did you start your own business?

Why did you decide to focus on what it is that you do and offer?

Why are you reading this book now?

Money may make the world go round, but it's never going to be enough to keep it spinning when you are having a bad day. Or want to go on holiday but can't afford to take the time off. Or want to go see your child's play that afternoon but you've two huge reports to finish off before 5pm.

There are lots of "get rich schemes" and "make money in your sleep" programs and systems you can buy into. But all they offer you, at best, is that short-term make-a-quick-buck.

Passive income is a phrase that I come across a lot. And it drives me potty. There is no such thing as passive income, you see. And the sooner you realise that you have to put some blood, sweat and tears into your business, the quicker you are going to realise the benefits.

And this is why you need to know your why.

Not every day is going to be great. You aren't going to achieve everything you strive for. You will get knock backs and rejections and clients demanding their money back because they didn't like what they got from you.

If you are only in it for the money, which I am sure you are not, then you will give up before you begin.

I have lots of reasons "why". The two biggest are my children. Without them, I wouldn't have been able to jump off that corporate cliff (without a parachute it felt like at the time) and have the excuse to go work for myself.

I want to have the freedom to work when I want and be a mum when I can. I couldn't do that in corporate life so creating a business around my skills and passions works.

So, what are your whys?

## Dig deep

Be truthful with yourself and get clear on the true whys. Without this, you will give up when you can't get your head around your autoresponder system or you won't find the time to re-write your sales page for your latest product. You will put off projects such as creating another free offer to build your list and product ideas will be left forgotten because you've drifted along to the end of another month with nothing much to show.

## Share with your loved and trusted ones

Don't share with everyone. Don't risk being scorned or scoffed at by people who don't believe in you. You run the risk of giving up before you've even started.

But do share with the right people who will encourage and push you when you doubt yourself. I've told my children that I am taking us all to Florida Disney during autumn half term. Now, that's an incentive for me to keep myself on the straight and narrow, I can tell you. They aren't going to let me forget that "why."

## Get visual

Whether you prefer to write, draw, cut out and stick, it's up to you. You can even create your own video to play at the start of each day. The more you see, hear and touch your "whys," the more likely you are going to keep them at the front of your mind. Essential when the going gets tough.

---

**MAGPIE ALERT**

*Just because I've mentioned the word video, don't get carried away and spend the next four days creating the next Spielberg blockbuster. Clarity is one thing, but taking up the best part of your week faffing about with some video editing tool is a time-suck.*

---

Some of the stuff that you are going to read in this book may feel like a mountain too big to climb. It may seem too much like hard work and way too much effort. But if you have your whys clearly set out and know exactly what you are aiming for, I promise you that you will be pleased you've gone the extra mile.

I don't want to see you having a dusty looking Facebook Page, a deserted Twitter account and an out-dated YouTube channel sitting in your nest doing nothing for your business.

Nor do I want to see you wasting your time, playing around and faffing about with your new, shiny toys, whilst your turnover and profit goes nowhere and your credit card debt increases.

Let's get on with it and work out how you can create the right marketing systems to get social media working for you in the right way.

## How to get the most out of this book

As you read through this book you will probably start to realise that this book is less about isolated social media strategies and more about online marketing. This is the reason why I decided that this book had to be written. There are so many books and teaching programmes on offer to you that will show you how to be successful on social media, but very few will show you how to integrate your social media marketing into the rest of your marketing strategy.

Social media marketing will not be successful when done as an isolated activity. If you want to "do it like the gurus do" and think you can put up a few videos on to YouTube, post a couple of updates to Facebook and expect your message to be spread globally in a few weeks ... think again.

It is easy to get sucked into all the "turnkey" products and shortcuts to success programmes. To get social media working for you and attracting the right clients constantly and consistently throughout the year, there is some groundwork and setting up of marketing systems to be done first.

And this is what this book will show you. Step One starts you right at the beginning and gets you to look at what target client you are focusing on. Steps Two and Three will show you how to get your house in order; your website and blog. Steps Four and Five are critical, as your email marketing and what you offer to convince your target clients to part with their contact details are your keys to unlocking your social media success. Step Six looks at how you set up and manage your social media and integrate it into your overall web marketing strategy. And finally, Step Seven shows how to truly shine.

It's up to you which chapter you read and when. I know that some of you will do the typical "read the last page to find out who's dunnit" and skip straight to Step Six.

That's fine by me. It's your business and your choice. But remember, a Facebook Page and Twitter account does not make a successful business; 10,000 fans and 55,000 followers does not necessarily guarantee fame and fortune.

It's all just ego.

If you want to know "who's dunnit" then start from the beginning and work your way through each step. If you read this book in the right order, then you will be the one who has dunnit. You will have the right web tech marketing tools working for you in the right way.

This is not a step-by-step manual that will show exactly all the buttons to press when. Social networks, in particular Facebook, change, take away and introduce new features continuously. If I were to focus on this side of "how to do social media" then this book would probably out of date within a few weeks.

More importantly, a step-by-step manual would more likely focus you on the shiny buttons themselves, rather than helping you decide what, why and how social media would work practically in your marketing.

I will be sharing plenty of short cuts, resources and ways of automating some of the marketing systems to make it easier for you to manage. But my role here is to take you up above the detailed tutorials – if you need this, then my Web Tech Club may just be the one-step resource that you are looking for - and help you think, plan and act on creating robust web based marketing systems that work consistently and constantly throughout your year.

Do you take action before moving on to each new step?

Well, yes that would be helpful. Reading this book alone will NOT make your business successful. It's the actions you take from the nuggets you get from reading this book that will make your business succeed. And never forget that. It's the same for every book you read on business, marketing and social media.

So read, absorb and read some more. You may even want to read this book from cover to cover to start with and then come back to each stage to take action.

But as I like to say to every client I work with … JFDI. (Google it if you don't know want it stands for.)

# STEP ONE
## YOUR CLIENT

Before you get stuck in to any form of marketing, web based or not, you have to take the time to *really* know your client first. Just because tools such as Twitter and Facebook are new, doesn't mean that basic marketing principles are thrown out of the window.

"But I don't have any clients. How am I suppose to get to know them if I can't find any to talk to?"

OK, so maybe you are starting out. You haven't got a database. But that's still no excuse for not doing your groundwork first and there are plenty of ideas of how you go about researching and defining who it is you want to work with.

### Don't start with a telephone directory

With no clearly identified clients, it is like picking up the telephone directory and calling each and every person in the book by alphabetical order. Yes, there is a chance that someone, somewhere in that book will say "yes" but how long does this take, how much does this time cost you and how dreadfully dull would it be to do?

You have to be very specific about the client you want to attract and this means you have to beyond describing your target clients as, for example, "women." There seem to be a lot of coaches and trainers who like to focus their businesses on working with women but "women" is not a target client profile.

How many women do you think are living in your neighbourhood? How many women do you think are living in your town? Push this out to the global marketplace and, using "women" as a target audience, means that, if you wanted to focus your marketing activities to reach out to women, you are actually trying to communicate with almost half the world's population. And that's a whole lot of people you will end up trying to speak to ... you may as well start with your local telephone directory.

If "women" were to be your focus, then you need to be more specific. For example: women who have turned 40 and are having a confidence crisis about being a decade older; women who have just had their second child and are concerned about the environment; women who are looking for a new career in the IT industry.

All these "women" have very different wants and desires. The woman turning 40 and panicking about her age is not going to be that concerned about how she could be using terry towelling nappies and cut down on waste. Each woman will have a different way of living her life, use different words and tone and different styles of communicating.

### Niche Marketing and why it works for small business owners like you

For many of you who hear the word "niche", you probably shudder, frown or shake your head in despair. "But I want to help lots of people. If I niche, I'll close myself off to too many people," is a phrase I hear a lot.

I remember a gentleman who called me about launching his new book. He wanted to find out if I could teach him how to use social media to sell more copies and reach a wider audience. It was a "how-to" book on giving up smoking. He was convinced it could help everyone who wanted to give up. And he was probably right – the book could probably help most smokers wanting to give up.

But there lay his problem. By trying to tell everyone who wanted to give up smoking about his book, would mean mass communication and, quite frankly, probably an expensive campaign (his time as well as his money setting everything up). There is every chance the campaign would end doing nothing but creating an awful lot of noise that no one wanted to listen to.

In today's busy consumer world, there is too much noise for people to pay much attention to generalised messages such as "Want to give up smoking? Then buy this book." The competition would be fierce and it would be easy to disappear in the sea of mediocrity.

Trying to open yourself up to as many people as possible can actually work in reverse. And you'll end up attracting no one.

Focusing on specific groups of people, who share specific problems, can mean you actually help more people who truly get what you offer. The marketing process is easier, because you can create clearly defined messages on the right social networks that work to attract rather than chase and hard sell.

As you go through this step, you may find that your target client actually hates using Facebook but will readily connect and engage with you within LinkedIn.

Going back to this gentleman who called me up - I suggested that, for us to work together on a marketing plan for his book, he would need to be focused on exactly who he wanted as his customer. He just seemed to shudder, frown and shake his head down the phone at me.

"But I want to help lots of people. If I niche, I'll close myself off to too many people," he said.

We didn't end up working together, as you probably can guess.

Niche marketing works for small businesses. The more focused you are on the particular problem that you can solve, the easier it is to communicate and spread the word about the solutions you offer.

And this is even more important in the online world and social media. It's so easy to automate and mass produce articles, tweets and web links in all the popular social networking sites, but it can get so noisy that everyone, including the target clients you are trying to reach out to, end up switching you off.

Imagine a coach who has a background in teaching and happens to love the great outdoors. What if you came to their Facebook Page and they were posting about articles on general life coaching, coaching support for teachers, a special programme that helped school children study better and a few walking holidays combined with offers of one-to-one coaching sessions.

Phew! All that from one person? Really?

She may end up feeling very proud of the few thousand friends and fans she has attracted over the past few months but if a large percentage of these people have decided to hide her updates from their newsfeeds (easily done and lots of people do this) then her messages are being ignored without her even realising it.

Let me give you another example. Think back to the last time you needed your boiler serviced. Who did you use? A specialist gas registered boiler servicing company or the odd-job-man who offers to clean your gutters, re-paint your living room, fix and install bathrooms, trim your hedges as well as service your boiler?

If your odd-job-man comes highly recommended by your neighbours, then perhaps he is the "man for the job" – but looking through the Yellow Pages, he may not be your first point of call.

So, what about you? If you are competing with everyone else and not at the stage that all your customers are coming via the "highly recommended" route, then you may want to take another look at your marketing messages.

Are you an odd-job-man? Or are you a specialist?

## Working with your ideal client

Before we get you having a go at writing out exactly who you want to focus on working with and creating a client profile, it is important to consider who it is you want to attract in to your business.

Working for yourself gives you an amazing advantage of choosing exactly who it is you want to spend your time with. Back in PAYE days, you didn't really have a choice, did you? But running your own business means that you do.

Do you ever find yourself thinking any of these thoughts?

> "I wish my customers would pay their invoices on time. I am fed up with having to phone them up and remind them every month."

> "I am dreading working with David this week. He drives me up the wall with his incessant questions and nit-picking details."

> "Why can't my customers read the instructions on the box? I am getting bored in answering the same questions all the time and I just can't afford to spend any more time sorting out returned goods."

Unless you have ambitions on being the next Richard Branson or Michelle Mone, you may not have million pound turnover goals. You may be striving for a £80,000 turnover this year or creating £24,000 of profit. It may be that bringing in an extra £800 each month would be more than enough for you to be proud of yourself.

No matter how small or big you want your business to be, you couldn't possibly be able to work with or provide your product to every single person who had the money for what you offered. In the early years you just wouldn't have the infrastructure to deal with the orders or delivery.

## "I know, I need to work with people who have money"

This is a common mistake that many business owners make when coming up with their ideal client. If you want to grow your business quickly, it's easy to feel that you need to focus on clients who have money to spend.

This is flawed in many ways.

1) You are making assumptions about what budget people have to spend.

2) People with spare cash to spend often spend it more wisely than others with not a lot; therefore they often haggle and have very high expectations (it's why they have lots of spare cash.)

3) If someone wants and desires something enough, they will go out of their way to find the money to spend with you. And, believe me, it's these clients who will truly value what you do and offer.

If you attract the people who you want to spend your time with, they are more likely to be customers who value you and your business. They will be more likely to pay your invoices on time, more likely to agree to a plan of action and stick to it and more likely to buy something that will add value to their lives.

When you come to write out your client profile, imagine yourself waking up on a Monday morning. You get yourself ready for business and you make your way to your waiting room.

### Imagine

Imagine your very own personal waiting room. It's decorated in exactly the style you dream of, with quality pictures on the wall, expensive furniture and a smiling receptionist greeting you with your favourite morning beverage.

Your waiting room is full. You've got people sitting, standing and perched on chair arms. Every person is different and they are waiting to see you.

You look around the room and you look each person in the eye. Who would you smile at and say to "Yes please, I think I would like to work with you today?"

Go on ... after you've read the questions below, close your eyes and imagine.

What does this person look like? How are they wearing their hair? What are they wearing? What's the colour of the shirt or blouse they have on? What shoes do they have? Are they casually dressed or wearing some form of uniform? What is their body language like? Are they meeting your eyes and looking straight back at you?

Now capture those images in your head and write the answers down.

This is the person you want to describe in your target client profile.

It can take a lot of courage to think of your potential customers in this way. You may even feel stupid allowing yourself this secret game of imagination. But who do you really want to spend time with each working week?

With people who drive you nuts with their nit picking and complaining? Or with people who love your products or spending time with you?

## Client profiling

To help you understand what are web tech tools and social media sites to use in your marketing and how you going to use them, your next step is to take the time to expand on your ideal client above and write out a detailed client profile.

The basic principle of profiling your client is to understand this person's personality and lifestyle. Client profiling can be exceptionally detailed and big brands and companies will spend hundreds and thousands investing in market research and focus groups that takes years and years of work.

Tesco is one of the giants in the UK retail sector and they invest millions. Their reward card gives them all the information they need to help build up pictures of how their customers spend their money and what they spend their money on – and not just in store, either. Tesco will track wherever a Tesco customer with a Tesco credit card spends their money.

But you don't have millions, do you? And you probably don't have years and years, either. You need to get to know your client quickly because if you don't, you could be wasting months of fiddling about in social networks and wasting your time creating a website that does nothing more than float around hyperspace, gathering pixel dust.

## Making assumptions

When you are first starting out with your client profile, you may have to make some assumptions. Social stereotyping is a useful way of approaching client profiling. For example, think in terms of how different types of people shop at different supermarkets.

If you are based in the UK, Waitrose is often perceived to be the most expensive supermarket. If we were to socially stereotype their customers we may think that their customers demand quality, organically grown produce and are concerned about the environment.

Asda is often perceived to be the value end of the market. Their customers think about special offers, three for two and keeping their weekly shopping costs down.

Be careful not to make too many sweeping assumptions, though. Times do change and people's shopping habits will change according to external factors such as the economy, job security and children growing up and leaving home.

If you are feeling stuck, then consider taking some form of market research.

## Market research for the small business owner

Market research sounds very corporate doesn't it? It's what the big companies do … it feels expensive and complicated. But market research doesn't have to cost you thousands and it doesn't have to take you months to do. Here are suggested short cuts and low cost ways of carrying out market research.

## Small sample

If you already have clients who have bought from you, select just a small sample to speak to individually. Pick out the people who have spent the most money with you, for example, and call them up on the phone.

## Online questionnaires

If you want to send out a questionnaire, you want to make it as easy and simple as possible to get as many people participating. Check out the resources page at the back for some suggested websites to look at that will offer you free ways of doing this.

### Interview key people

If you are starting with no clients or feel that the clients you have are not the ones you want to work with, ask your network for recommendations of people who fit the profile of person you wish to interview. Offer to buy them a cup of coffee and pick their brains for a short while.

Quick story to share with you. When I first started up as a life coach – back before the days of social media and blogging – I decided I wanted to specialise in the field of coaching professional mums back to the workplace. And I thought that focusing on professions such as accountancy and law would be a great field to work in.

My thought process was that it took so much time and money for firms to invest in qualified staff, that it made sense – to me – that they would want to spend money on coaching and mentoring mums back into the work force rather than lose them and their investment.

I set about interviewing some key professionals in the area. I interviewed Senior Law Partners. I met up with female managers. And I even got to sit down with a lady who was on maternity leave and question her about her plans and motivations.

To cut a long story short, all my research led me to the conclusion that what I wanted to offer was great … but no one wanted to pay for it. I had found something that people needed, but they didn't want nor desire enough to invest in what I was planning to offer at that time.

By doing this market research it saved me months of marketing that just wouldn't have worked. And it enabled me to focus my energies on something that women did want, which was helping them start up their own businesses.

Take these market research short cuts and low cost ways and see what you come up with. And always remember that time and money spent on market research is almost always time and money well spent.

As your business grows and you are able to invest in your future growth, investing in specialist market research help and support may be something you need to consider. But you have to start somewhere. And it is better to have 10 interviews or 30 responses to an online questionnaire to build from, than sitting in your home office guessing and making "wrong" assumptions.

**Corporate clients**

What if you plan to work with corporates?

Businesses and corporate clients are still made up of human beings. It is the human beings that make the decisions to speak to you over the phone, make the decisions to bring you into present your business case and make the decisions to spend the money with you.

Adjust your questions in your market research to reflect corporate life. For example, find out how the structure and line management works, who makes decisions at different levels and how these people view themselves.

Human Resources Managers tend to have different objectives to the MD. The gatekeepers – receptionists and Personal Assistants – will be motivated by different approaches than their Line Managers.

Same principles - just use different questions.

## The market research that's bad for business

When you are starting up your own business and deciding on a particular niche or specialty to focus on, one of the mistakes that many small business owners fall into is searching on the internet for people who do what you want to do already.

Now, of course it's important to check out your competition. It can be a useful yardstick to help you understand price ranges, services to offer and products that sell well.

BUT when that internet searching becomes endless hours of finding more and more websites, all seemingly to be offering a bigger and better service/product that you could even dream about – then STOP!

Worrying about your competition at such an early stage can be damaging to your confidence levels. In today's market place it is highly unlikely to "discover" a unique niche. You should be more worried that no one is doing what you want to be doing because it generally means there is no demand – but that's a lesson for another book.

**MAGPIE ALERT**

*Internet searching sucks you in ... for hours at a time. If you do need to do some Google searching around your niche and target client, then set a timer to cut you off after thirty or forty minutes. If you want to save certain websites for future reference, go back to the section "Managing your ideas and resources" to use one of the recommended approaches.*

## More than one client profile

You may feel that you have lots of different client profiles within your business. Yes, it is true you may find that a whole range of different people can buy your product or service.

But beware the "More is Better." A scattergun approach to your marketing will leave you feeling poor, exhausted and demoralised. The more focused you are on a particular niche, the more effective your communications will be within tools such as blogs and social media.

It is far more effective use of your time and your money to focus your proactive marketing activities on one client profile at a time. Your messages will be clearer and the relationships that you build will be stronger.

By all means have different client profiles that you want to build over time, but build one at a time and you will see greater results from your marketing activities.

## Creating your target client profile

On the next few pages you will find lists of questions for you to answer. There are two parts to writing out your target client profile. Part One is about building a lifestyle profile – understanding the personality of the ideal customer. And part two is building a psychological profile; delving a little deeper and understanding their problems.

When answering the questions during this first part be as specific as you can be. The more detail you give yourself, the more likely you are to understand what makes this person tick and it will help you in Part Two.

You will notice that with some of the questions you will probably never truly know the answer. Make assumptions. Socially stereotype. Create that picture that you need to help shape your messages and decide which web tech marketing tools to use.

It's important to take time out of your busy week to do this. Don't do this on the fly. Switch the phone to answer machine, close down your email and shut your office door. This is a "Do Not Disturb" zone. (Remember reading about managing your interruptions earlier in this book?)

If you find this hard to do by yourself, consider finding a business buddy who will ask you the questions. Having someone else asking the questions can sometimes help trigger thoughts and they often ask other questions that you may not have thought of.

If you do want to use a business buddy, do make sure you are comfortable with answering their questions and that they are non-judgmental in their question asking. If they think they know about the target client you want to describe, they may end up asking leading questions and may cloud your thought process.

## Giving your target client a name

Giving your target a name can be really helpful in personalising them and making then "real". You will find it easy to write your communications – emails, status updates, blog posts – when thinking of one person, instead of a whole group.

It's only a bit of fun and not something that you would use in your actual marketing messages, but it can really help trigger your writing and messages. So go on, first question to answer: what's your client called?

## Part One – Lifestyle profile

Imagine yourself walking into your waiting room again. Who did you smile at, look into their eyes and say "Yes please, I want to work with you today?" Write down the initial thoughts that have come into your head.

Use the questions below to help you create more detail about this person.

- Where do they live?

- What sort of house do they live in?

- What car do they drive?

- Where do they shop?

- Where do they go on holiday?

- Who do they work for or with? Or what do they do?

- How much do they earn?

- How do they earn their money?

- What else would you need to know to help you be totally clear on who your ideal customer would be?

- Where do they hang out online? Are there specific niche forums where they join in with discussions? Or do they rarely use the internet?

- How do they like to communicate? Do they love email and hate text? Or prefer stuff through the post?

- Which social networks do they like to use? And why?

**Some example questions to ask if you are targeting a business or corporate client** (and some of these you will most certainly not want to assume ... ask and do your market research here)

- Who makes the actual decisions within the business?

- What sort of people do you have to speak to before you get to talk to the decision maker?

- What is important to each of these people?

- What goals or targets does each of these people have within the business?

- How do these people get paid and if they are on commission, what affects their final salary?

- What lifestyle does each of these people have outside of the business?

**Part Two – Psychological profile**

This next step is about getting "under the skin" of your client. The psychological make-up of a person will help you understand the ways to communicate with them, when to communicate with them and what you end up saying to them when you do communicate.

The more you understand about how your customer communicates, the better copy you will write for your website, your blog articles and newsletters and use the right trigger words on your social networking profiles.

- What problems does your customer have?

- What thoughts and anxieties keep them awake at night?

- How does your customer feel about these problems?

- What solutions do you offer to overcome these problems?

- What makes you different from your competitors?

These last two questions start to really take your client profiling to the next level and will help you start to understand what you need to do and what you need to be in order to be different and stand out from all the rest.

There are so many blah blah businesses using social media, that their messages just get ignored. If you want to avoid getting ignored and passed over, then give these questions some serious thought.

If you really find yourself struggling, then this is where a business coach or mentor can make a huge difference to your success. It is something I do a lot with clients before helping them with their social media strategies. And having an external person who is independent from your business can really help bring out the answers from within you.

**Needs v Wants: Why do your clients really spend their money with you?**

I don't want to deviate from the topic of social media marketing but there is one more classic marketing concept that needs addressing before you set up your web marketing systems; the confusion between thinking what your target clients needs and what they really want.

Let me tell a quick story (and I am sure this has happened to you a lot, too). I popped into a local branch of Waitrose the other week for a couple of pints of milk and a few veggies. Now the thing about food shopping in the likes of Waitrose and M&S (two of the UK's leading top-nosh retailers) is that it is very easy to get caught up and turn your five item list into an over-loaded shopping trolley.

I came out with a couple of frozen pizzas (to top up my last-minute-supper freezer draw,) bag of chicken breasts (they were on special offer so I saved £2.31,) a selection of frozen herbs (3 for £4 – how can I refuse?) and a punnet of strawberries (over-priced and out-of-season but remembered my 10 year old mentioning he wanted strawberries on the way to school) to name but a few things that I wanted – but I didn't really "need."

My quick shop became £69.54, which was precisely £50 more than I had intended to spend.

Why did I spend so much more than I intended?

The £50 was the difference between buying what I "wanted" and buying what I "needed".

Many of you assume what you think your target clients want, when in fact you are actually deciding what you think they "need". Yes, some people "need" help with their time management.  But do they "want" to spend their money (and their time) on a half day workshop or three month long training programme to improve it?

Some people "need" to organise their house and de-clutter their cupboards, but do they "want" to cough up a few hundred pounds for someone to come in and do it for them?

And yes, there are people who "need" to lose weight, feel more confident, find a perfect partner and know how to manage their staff better – but if they don't "want" to pay for a solution then it's doesn't matter how much your service is "needed," you won't find enough clients unless your solution is something they "want."

By making sure your solutions – your products, services, programmes or events – are designed and packaged in a way so that they are desired and "wanted," you will see better results in your social media marketing.

Go back through your target client profile and make sure you have truly understood what your target clients want and what they truly desire … not what you think they need.

If you can't confidently swear on your smart phone that you really do know (or you find that the products you are creating are just not getting any interest from your target clients) then you will need to go back a step and carry out some all-important market research.

## What do you do with the clients who you aren't targeting?

You probably wouldn't want to turn down clients who came to you who weren't your targeted client. After all, in the early stages of starting your own business, you may need the money and cash flow is king when you run your own business.

But your marketing approach and the way that you communicate with people should reflect your USP and your chosen niche.

Those clients who don't fit your profile could provide you with some useful feedback for future business development.

These are some useful questions to ask yourself:

- Why do you feel you are attracting these people?

- Does your product or service mean something else to other people?

- Does it create an opportunity that you hadn't previously considered?

A word of caution though – keep focused on your original marketing plan and only change direction once you are clear on what your plan should be. Flitting from one target group to another every other month will not only be confusing for you but will also confuse your potential clients.

## Where next?

The more you know about your target client, the easier the rest of your plan is going to be. And I will be referring back to this step time and time again through the rest of this book.

If your clients don't use a particular social tool, why go through the pain of setting one up? You don't need to be a magpie. Be what's right for your clients first and foremost.

Time to move on to Step Two and getting your house in order.

# STEP TWO
# YOUR WEBSITE

Every business should have a website, right?

Absolutely!  Every business, big or small, should have some sort of web presence.  The internet is part of everyday life and, as you don't need thousands of pounds to get a business online now, there really is little excuse for a business not to a have a website created at some point.

But is your current website a help or a hindrance?

Just because you're online, doesn't necessarily mean it's doing anything for you.  And there's every chance your website could actually be working against you.

Let's look at how the average person uses the web. Did you know that the average time it takes for someone to "read" a website is three seconds?

Think back to the last time you used Google to find something.  You may have been looking for the best place to buy toner cartridges for your printer. It could have been that you were trying to find a villa or cottage to rent for your holiday next year.

Do you remember how long you took to make the decision to hit that back button and go on to the next website on the search results listings?  I am pretty sure it took you less than that average of three seconds on the websites that didn't grab you.

How long would it take for a visitor landing on your home page right now to make a decision to stay or go? One minute? Ten seconds? Or less than the average three seconds?

And imagine if they were on hold to their bank at the time, or waiting for a file to download on to their laptop, whilst they click through to your website. People often multi-task whilst searching on the internet so there's every chance you won't have their full attention as they land on your website. Is your website up for this tough job?

It could be that your website is being more of a hindrance, than a help. Here are some of the common "hindrances" that I see every day on websites that don't generate any leads or new clients for a business.

**A website that talks about the company and not the potential customer.** Take a look at your home page and count up every "we", "I" and your company name. Now count up the words that relate to your client; words such as "You" or "Your."

What's the ratio? I am expecting it to be about 75% in favour for "we", "I" and your company name and just 25% for "you" and "your." Don't worry, this is a very common problem; businesses are "wee-ing" all over the internet every day.

But it should be the other way around. Your clients are only interested in themselves when they are looking for someone to help them. If your website is just telling them how brilliant you are and what you do, they just won't care. What's in it for them?

(More about copy writing for your website in a little while.)

**A website that is obviously homemade.** You may have gone on a HTML programming course to save yourself a few pennies. You may have even used your next-door neighbour's son who is studying IT at Uni. But, saving money on your website to end up with a site that doesn't work in a particular browser or doesn't display on a mobile phone, will only push clients away.

There is really little excuse not to have a nicely designed website. Using blog platforms such as WordPress.org, for example, mean that you can have a simple, professional looking site that works, set up for as little as £300 to £750, depending on how much design time is involved. (More about website platforms in a little while.)

**A website that has a fussy design, clashing colours and is more concerned with how pretty or trendy it looks.** Internet users want to find their information quickly. They don't want to hunt for it in cleverly worded menus or images. Flash introductions just annoy most people – remember the three second time limit. Unless your clients expect to watch a dancing cartoon or slideshow, they will be gone before it has finished playing.

Flash images (and I mean moving graphics rather than flashy designs) don't translate well on most smartphones and tablets either. They don't work at all on Apple based devices such as iPhones and iPads. If your objective is to start using social media in your marketing, you've got to make sure you have a mobile friendly website as much of your social network will be using their smart phones when clicking through to your website from your profile links and updates.

**A website with no obvious purpose.** Static brochure style websites just don't "do" anything. They may look pretty and give lots of information, but what are you expecting your website visitor to do once they land on your website? A typical coaching or training website will have, at best, a "call me now on xxx" somewhere at the bottom of their home page. That is their only call to action. Sorry, but picking up the phone and making an enquiry cold from a website is just too big a leap to make for most of your clients. This is just not good enough if you want to have your website working as a marketing tool.

I do rant on about this point the most, to be honest. It happens a lot, especially if you, the business owner, goes to a website designer who isn't trained to be a marketer. Most website designers are technically trained, coming from either a programming or graphic design background. Having the skill of a marketer is a lot to ask, so it is your job as the business owner, to make sure you take responsibility for this.

You may be lucky and find a website designer with great SEO skills (search engine optimisation). Getting your website found on Google is important as you shouldn't rely on using the likes of social media to direct people there. But again, having a well optimised site, doesn't mean a jot if your site has no clear call to action once someone finds it.

A lot of website designers want to produce beautiful pieces of art; they focus their efforts on colours, design and clever images to make your site look different. Branding and design is important and if you can find a website designer to create something like this that you are happy with, then great. But don't get caught up with the design and forget about your marketing objectives.

---

**MAGPIE ALERT**

*Decorating your house is always more fun than spending money on essential works such as electrics or new central heating system. But there's nothing worse than having your freshly painted kitchen and interior designed living room flooded one morning because your ancient water pipes just burst. Magpies love to decorate their nest but if the nest is not built with strong foundations to start with, it won't be any good when it's time to hatch your eggs.*

---

First and foremost, your website has to be a marketing tool. You have to be clear about your objectives and what part you want it playing in your web marketing systems. It has to do its job and that job is to convert website visitors into paying clients.

To spend your hard earned money and time creating a website just so potential clients can "find out more about you" is a waste. You are throwing money away. Your website will just float around in hyperspace, gathering pixel dust and often ends up being ignored by anyone who happens to stumble upon it.

There are only two clear goals for your website and they are to 1) sell your products there and then or 2) to capture contact details.

Unless you are a retail business selling craft products, kids clothes or laptop cases, then you need to create a website that captures contact details. Selling coaching, training or any other kind of service cold from a website is tough.

And if you are not including some way of asking potentially interested visitors to leave their name and email address and get added to your mailing list, then just get your coat. The party is over for you and you may as well go home.

List building is a critical part of your web marketing systems and there's much, much more about this very topic in Steps Four and Five later on in this book. But for now, let's get back to your website.

**Getting your nest in order**

In the first step outlined in this book, you spent some time getting clearer on who you want to reach out to? Before you start inviting people to your party, you've got to make sure your venue is up for it. You don't decide to celebrate a big birthday with one hundred of your friends and family in your back garden if it's no bigger than a picnic blanket, do you?

Nor would you contemplate a posh six-course dinner party if the only table you have is a rickety old kitchen table that's big enough just for you and the cat.

## Client expectations are high

We all expect a lot today, don't we? You want a good price and you also expect quality service. Ten years ago – even just three or four years ago – you could get away with a basic, homemade website. But today, you've got to look professional, trustworthy and credible if you want potential clients coming from your website.

It's all about trust. Your clients don't want to get spammed. They don't want to get their credit cards scammed. And they don't want to run the risk of catching and downloading a virus. If your site looks and feels untrustworthy in any way, your potential clients will be off.

You wouldn't turn up to a local business networking event in your gardening or dog walking clothes, either. You may not be a suited-and-booted kind of person, but you would put on a clean shirt, brush your hair and make sure your shoes weren't scuffed at the very least, wouldn't you? It's the same with your website. Homemade graphics and a snap shot of you on holiday in Cornwall two years ago, is not exactly going to represent you in a professional and business like way.

Even if you are offering services and products within sectors that don't want the corporate look, such as the spiritual, environmental or ethical market places, you still have to create an image that people will trust and feel happy with spending money with you.

Your clients also expect to find you online. They will Google your name, your business name and any other key words that you may be associated with. If they can't find you online or get what they are looking for on your website, you've lost your opportunity to win over a new client.

All this doesn't mean you have to be thinking of spending thousands to develop a top of the range, flashy looking website; actually, far from it. Today, there are plenty of website tools available to business owners like yourself that will allow you to get a professional and effective website at a good price.

So, before you start getting busy in Facebook or tweeting away, sort out your party venue and get your house in order.

**Can't you just go and set up a Facebook Page and do away with all the hassle of building your own website?**

A lot of business owners are beginning to ask this. If it's all happening over in the likes of Facebook, why not set up your home over there?

Last year there was yet another uproar in the Facebook communities. Facebook were making changes to the Business Pages and after a nine minute outage, the new look Page had gone as quickly as it appeared. (In fact, you could be reading this book in years to come and this story will still be up to date and relevant ... Facebook is always making changes so always be prepared.)

"How dare they change the format of the Pages" was one comment I read.

"Don't they know it businesses like ours that pay their salaries – I'm not going to advertise if they take away my welcome page" was another.

Why the uproar? The new look Page had moved the tabs to a left hand menu and had taken away the ability to set a default welcome page for "non-likers." Lots of businesses have invested several hundred pounds (if not more) to get this page designed to incorporate opt-in boxes to their mailing lists and persuade the first time visitor to their page to like them.

(This feature of setting your default welcome page has not returned, you will be pleased to know. More of this in more detail in the social media chapter, Step Six.)

The problem in all of their complaints is that Facebook is free. None of us pay or subscribe to their services, unless you choose to advertise on their site. Do any of us have the right to complain?

And here lies an even bigger problem – especially if you are relying on Facebook to market your business.

*Never make Facebook (or any other social network) your home.*

If Facebook or any other social network is the central hub of your marketing and you are relying on it to build your business, it makes it a very dangerous place for you to be; especially when they all keep changing their terms of services, features and rules of engagement.

Facebook should always be your welcome mat – a place to direct and invite interested people to find out more in your own home. Your own home is your website and your blog. These are the places you can control and these should always be the central hub to your marketing.

### What your website should be and do

I've written a lot about all the mistakes you guys are making with your websites, but let's get on with what you should be having and doing with your website. What does your website need to be and do?

**Meet your business objectives**: Don't start any website project until you have decided exactly what your website is there to do for you. If all you want is a brochure, then expect it to be found only by the people you send the links to. Make sure you set the goal of either selling direct for retail or collecting email addresses for service based services and products.

**Use a flexible and adaptable website platform that can grow with you.** Gone are the days that a website designer has to spend days programming and writing script to create a website. Yes, there are going to be certain projects that need high level programming – ecommerce sites, corporate extranets – but for most of you reading this book, your website can be built from templates and easy to use content management software.

You really don't need to know how to use FTP (file transfer protocol which is the software that allows you to upload files to your web hosting) or complicated HTML code (the language used to write the code for many websites.)

Blogging is covered in detail in the next step, but whether you want to be blogging or not, doesn't matter at this stage. This is because the best platforms to build a website that is flexible and adaptable enough to grow with you are blogging platforms.

It is why I love and recommend WordPress.org so much. It's free – yup, FREE – to download and although I would never recommend non-technical people to set up a WordPress.org website from scratch, once someone has set up the design templates, created the pages and menu, you can edit and manage your own website as easily as using a word document.

(**Note:** *from now on, when referring to WordPress.org, I will only use the phrase WordPress.*

*Some people do get confused between
WordPress.org and WordPress.com. WordPress.com
is a self-hosted version where you can create a
website/blog more simply and easily than using the
WordPress.org files.*

*As a business owner, it is not recommended you use
the WordPress.com version. You want to own,
manage and control your own website rather than
have it owned by another company, which is the
case with WordPress.com – read the small print of
their terms of business. The day that your
WordPress.com website gets shut down because
you have inadvertently contravened their terms of
service, will not be one your favourite moments)*

**Focus on your target audience**. Too often a website
is trying to be everything to everyone.  If you are
trying to engage with finance professionals on
Twitter, then make sure the website that listed on
your Twitter profile takes them to a website that is
all about working with finance professionals.

Does that mean that you may have more than one
website? Well, yes. That is often the case. If you
have taken the time to work out your niche and
profiled your ideal target client, don't go wasting all
that work on spreading your bets and covering all
your bases.

If you've found you want to work with several client
profiles, then you will find that it will be more
effective and more profitable for you to create
separate websites for each target client. If this feels
all rather overwhelming, check out the section

coming on buying dedicated domains. It could be helpful for you to start off with one website and give you time to build up your cashflow – and mental space – then to go forth and create more websites.

**Speak the right language.** Twitter and Facebook are very social networks. They are relaxed and friendly. If the links from your updates and online profiles send them through to a stiff, corporate website, it may present too big a leap for someone to feel they have found what they are looking for.

Your copy and style certainly doesn't need to be texted based, 140 character based tweets. But you if step out of a warm hot bath into a cold shower, then you are going to jump out again very quickly.

**It is all about you and not the corporate logo.** As you will be reading more on how you should engage on social networks, you need to be "you" when you are posting your updates.

Going from someone's twitter feed who tweets about life as a solopreneur or a mum working from home, to a website that talks about the "royal we" and avoids any mention of being a small business, is just not going to be congruent to your online brand.

**You've got to be up to date.** An events page with workshops listed from 4 months ago just looks bad. A "latest news" page with a press release from 2009 is lazy. Get your events updated ... or take the page down.

**Clear navigation**: Most websites have navigations across the top or left hand column. It's what most online users are used to. Now is not the time to try to be different. If your target customers can't find what they are looking for, they will leave your site. Pure and simple.

This also applies to what you call your options on your menu bar. If you offer services, products and events, but refer to them as "coaching" "store" and "come meet us", you run the risk of confusing even the most sensible of people. Call your pages "services" "products" and "events." As Ronseal say, do what it says on the tin.

**Professional design**: As mentioned already, graphic design need not cost the earth, especially when using cheap templates to start your design from. But skimp on professional advice and you could end up with a tacky looking homemade effect that will destroy all your marketing efforts.

---

*MAGPIE ALERT*

*DIY design can really drag you down. Deciding on the exact pantone shade of purple to use is really not best use of your time. Your clients won't care.*
*Fact! Good is good enough and striving for a perfect design is commercial suicide, especially if you are doing it yourself. You have been warned.*

---

**Appropriate images**: Avoid the obvious ones (stack of pebbles or women standing on top of mountain with open arms that all life coaches seem to have) however, there are good online photo libraries to look at and find images starting from as little as $1. Check out the resources page to see the sites that I regularly use.

A picture is worth a thousand words so find images that emphasise your copy and helps make your message stand out. If the image doesn't add anything to help engage with your target client and make them feel they've come to the right site, then don't use it.

**Well written copy**: And the best to last. It doesn't matter how beautifully designed your logo and site is, or how artful your images are … if your words don't hit your target clients right between the eyes, draw them in and persuade them to take up your call to action, your website will fail.

### Copywriting: your golden ticket to web marketing success

Unfortunately, copy for your website is usually the task that is left to last when most business owners get their websites designed. My website designer I used to use, back before the days of using WordPress, used to tell me the number one reason why websites took so long to get finished was because the business owner couldn't get their act together with the copy.

There's a panic. You don't know what you should be writing. You probably hate writing, as it's not a natural skill for most of us, so you put it off and put it off until the last minute. You finally rush through some ideas on a Friday afternoon because you just have to get your website live and email them over to your website designer.

Your website designer is not a copywriter. They won't tell you whether it is OK or not. All they care about is whether the site works and meets the design and functionality brief you have lined out. So, the site goes live … and fails.

The copywriting you have rushed through on a Friday afternoon does nothing to "sell" your call to action and yup, is just "wee-ing" all over the internet. So, what to do?

Writing is a skill that you can develop. Honestly, you probably feel you can't write right now. I didn't think I could when I first started in business. I hated writing copy and found coming up with articles for my newsletter incredibly arduous. In fact, if I look back on my first attempt of home page copy, it really is quite laughable. But writing great copy is a skill; just like driving a car or riding a bicycle. You can learn.

I highly recommend that you read about the topic of business writing whenever you can. Grab any opportunity you can to practice, practice and practice. If there were just one book to recommend to you to get you started, it would be "Yes! 50 secrets from the science of persuasion" co-authored by Robert Cialdini. It really explains the psychology behind selling and helps you understand the power of using certain words and turns of phrases.

If you really can't do it – then outsource the work. Never, ever have a website that can't sell for you without you.

Here are some copy writing tips to get you on the right path.

**It's never about you but always about your clients.** Avoid the trap of writing about yourself and your business because ultimately your potential clients will only care about what's in it for them.

So what if you are the market leaders in your region – what does that mean to your client? So what if you have worked with all the big names – how does that benefit your client? Don't list the reasons why you are so great. Focus on the benefits to your clients.

**Stop writing "we" and start writing "you".** I've already suggested you do this, but I will suggest it again. This time, take action and change the copy.

Print out your home page copy and highlight every "we", "our" and reference to your business name. Then highlight every "you" in a different colour. There should be five times as many "you"s as there are "we"s – but you'll probably find the opposite.

For every sentence that has a "we" or an "our" in it, re-write it and change the reference to a "you" and you'll be on the right track to having copy that engages with your potential client, rather than turns them off.

For example: "We run fun, energising sessions that everyone loves" becomes "You will find you can't help but smile during our sessions and you will be buzzing with energy for days after an afternoon with us."

Another example" "Our training days turn mediocre sales people into top performers within a week" becomes "Your sales teams are turned into top performers within a week of attending one of our training days, meaning that you will see a 27% increase in your product sales this month."

Subtle differences, but these changes would make a huge difference to the target client who will be reading it.

**Quantify and qualify.** You'll notice I added a very brave 27% in the example above. If you can prove and qualify specific results, for goodness add this to your website copy. Don't chicken out with words such as "better" or "stronger." Be specific with your quantities. Avoid rounding up and rounding down, too. 27% just sounds more real than 30% doesn't it?

**Speak your client's language – not your own.** It's easy to use industry standard pre-fixes and jargon when writing your website copy. After all, you probably use these words every day when you talk to colleagues or suppliers.

But your clients probably don't. Use words they wouldn't understand and you'll end up alienating them at worst or coming across too corporate at best.

I remember a recruitment consultant who I used to manage back in my corporate days. He used to take great pleasure in using long words that he felt showed off his intellect. For example, he would use the word "eponymous" for describing a company called British Gas on a candidate's CV. A client being forwarded this CV would know what a company called British Gas would do, so there was absolutely no need to use a pompous word like "eponymous" on a CV. (Eponymous means that the words explain themselves – it is a lovely word to say, but rather arrogant when used in writing copy, don't you think?)

A great way of bringing your clients language into your website copy is to use phrases and words that your clients use when you do your market research. Make a special note of writing down the exact phrases when you interview people and use these in your copywriting.

Your inbox is another great resource. I will often tag particular emails from specific clients and subscribers to my newsletters and store them in a folder that I can go back to and research what specific words to use. For example, client and customer mean the same thing but different businesses use one or the other. If I was writing this book aimed at retailers who were looking to understand how to use social media effectively, I would use the word "customer" throughout this book. As this book is aimed at coaches, trainers and consultants, you view your customers as "clients."

**Correct grammar of course, but don't be afraid of writing colloquially.** If your potential clients use informal language, then embrace it. If they use slang, embrace it too.

Over the years, I have had the odd email from a subscriber pointing out my occasional spelling mistakes and bad grammar. Oh how I love to get these. But for most of you, the feedback has been that you've enjoyed my natural "speaking" style – I write how I talk. If it works for your potential clients, then use it.

**Use short paragraphs, bullet points and selective bolding.** Reading from a screen is different from reading the printed page. People tend to scan and often don't read word for word.

Make it easier for your online visitor to digest your words by using one to three sentence paragraphs; even consider using just three or four words per paragraph to really emphasise a point.

Break it up with bullet points where appropriate. And use bold and italics selectively (too much & it defeats the object.)

**To create action you need to demonstrate pain.** Your potential client will only contact you to spend money with you (I'm not including the freebie hunters who ask for advice but aren't prepared to pay for your time to receive it) if they find themselves in enough pain. That pain could be confusion and loss of direction or losing profitability and sales – if there's no pain, why would they spend money with you to solve a problem they don't have?

To identify a reason to contact you, they need to identify with the problems you highlight in your website copy. Remember the differences between what you think your target clients "need" and what they really "want"? It is critical you focus on the "wants" at this stage, as it will make sure you are offering to solve the right problem.

Don't just focus on the pleasure all the time and write warm, fuzzy words. Yes, you want your clients to feel good about themselves, don't you? But if you don't tell them and remind them about how bad – really, bad – the pain is for them, they may just not be motivated enough to pick up the phone, send you an email or opt-in to your free offer.

Hit them where it hurts and create enough reason for them to follow through on your call to action.

**Copywriting is THE one skill that will make or break you**

I am not expecting to have turned you into an expert copywriter in this chapter; however I hope I have given you enough tips and suggestions to get you on the right path.

If there were one skill that I recommend you spend as much time and money developing, it would be copywriting. It's the one area that is the toughest – and most expensive – skill to outsource and if you can write well and sell from your written words, your business is guaranteed of success.

## Dedicated domains

Remember me mentioning a little while ago the need for different websites for different target clients? I know that may have sounded rather daunting and a lot like hard work, especially if you haven't even started your first website.

You may also be in the position that you have several programmes, products or specific events on offer that are getting rather lost, being housed under one roof.

Whether you plan to have several niches or several products, programmes or events, it may not be practical or profitable to be creating separate websites at this time.

No problem. Dedicated domains can be a great short cut to having lots of mini-sites and other websites created, as well as keeping your online visitor within your one site.

Let me give you an example. You may be promoting a particular workshop called "Creative Minds."

You have the page on your website listing the dates, times, agenda and testimonials but that page url may be something like

this: www.YourBizName.co.uk/workshops/feb/
creativeminds.html

That's quite a link if you are using this page to send
people to in your marketing, even if you are using
the url shorteners that the likes of Twitter give you.

(**Note:** *Url shorteners are services that provide
exactly that service. You paste your long url into a
form, click convert and the url shortener service
turns it into a shorter url. For example http://sn.im/
49f056. If you create a free account, you also have
the option of creating bespoke urls, as long as no
one else has claimed them. For example, http://
sn.im/creative.*

*Each social network will tend to use their own url
shortener whenever you want to reduce a long link
within a tweet or status update. If you can avoid
using url shorteners, do. Many web savvy users will
not click them as spam users use them a lot to get
access to your accounts via phishing viruses.*

*For example "Wow, you look amazing http:bit.ly/
ditwq994 is pretty much guaranteed to be a
phishing link (I'm afraid, it's not real) So avoid these
when you see these types of tweets come through
in your newsfeeds. Avoid even when they are from
a reputable person as it could be that they clicked
on a similar account, have now been hacked and
the system is now automatically sending out tweets
via their account. You don't want it to happen to
your account, too.)*

If a link is too long it runs the risk of being easily
broken when forwarded and shared with others.
Plus, these sorts of links don't look too good on a

printed leaflet and far too long for people to remember if you are telling them.

Register a domain such as www.CreativeMinds.co.uk – something short and snappy which people can type easily – and set up your web host to re-direct the traffic to the dedicated page on your website. This should be fairly straightforward and is usually set from the control panel when you log in to the website where you have bought your domain from.

---

**MAGPIE ALERT**

*If re-directing urls sounds too complicated for you to do, then don't attempt this yourself. Contact who ever has done your website and ask them to sort this. This should be an easy task for them to sort out for you.*

---

If you want to use this practice to help direct one target client to one page on your website and another target client to another page, you could use these dedicated domains to send people to different landing pages on your website, rather than automatically sending them to your rather less focused home page.

You may even want to create a squeeze page, which is a page on your website that is not part of your navigation and the person visiting that page has only one action to take; usually subscribe or buy something that you are offering.

If I've just made your head explode, which may have just happened if all these concepts are new to you, don't worry. You will be reading more about squeeze pages in Steps Five when we look at offering free reports in more detail. Squeeze pages are very useful tools to have in your kit bag ... definitely not just a shiny toy.

**How many clicks to find your contact details?**

One of the most frustrating things that a potential new client may have about your website is finding out how to talk to you. Your target client has clicked through to your website from a link you've posted on one of your social networks, they like what you have to offer and they interested in spending money with you. They've just got a couple of quick questions to ask first but ... how do they get in touch with you?

Yes, yes, yes, so you've got a "Contact Us" page. But if your telephone number or email address is more than one click away from the page a potential client is on, then it's one click too many.

It's a real danger for a business, especially a service based business that is selling "you," to go down the online route, start promoting themselves on social media sites and then try to be "too online."

How many times have you found yourself wanting to phone someone up before placing an online order? You are on a specific page on someone's website, you want to check a particular size or clarify a colour and you don't want to click away and run the risk of not finding that page again. But you can't see a phone number or email address anywhere. Frustrating isn't it?

Enquiry forms and "contact us" forms are important. There will be lots of people who will prefer to use these rather than phone you up or email you. But how many times have you wanted to ask a quick question there and then? There's something still very instinctive about wanting to speak to a human being and if you can't find that all important telephone number to call that human being, you may well be losing out on that potential enquiry or sale.

## It's a trust thing

Being able to contact you by phone is a trust thing. If you hide behind "contact us" forms and cloaked email addresses and only list a PO Box address, then you aren't giving out the right signals to be trusted.

Oh a quick rant to all UK based businesses about 0845 numbers. Don't! Use your local code at all times. Many people are wary about calling these numbers – and all the rest such as 0871, 0843 and 0844 – because of the cost implications, especially from a mobile.

If you aren't based where you want to be targeting, then buy tracking phone numbers. You can buy any phone number in any part of the country, advertise this on your website or any part of your marketing and when someone dials this number, they are diverted to your main office number. Sweet.

Not only does this phone number give the impression of it being a local number, you can track exactly how many calls you get through on each number you use – hence the name "tracking numbers." These are particularly useful if you are planning a big campaign, both on and offline. You may use one tracking number for your Facebook Page, another for your sales page on your website, another for the leaflet that is being mailed out through the post and different tracking numbers for each of your adverts.

Suddenly, you are in control and see exactly which adverts, social networks and pages on your website gets you better results. It may be that you end up dropping your adverts and concentrate on your Facebook Page and direct mail leaflets because the adverts have failed, thus saving your money next time round.

Oh and whilst I am still in ranting mode about phone numbers, avoid listing just a mobile number, too. You may be mobile and always away from your desk (or it could be that you haven't got round to installing a dedicated business line into your home yet) but listing just mobile numbers looks amateurish and sometimes a little dodgy. If you are in business and mean business then get a dedicated business line coming into your house.

You shouldn't be too available either. Use an answering service to take your calls if you are out and about most of the time. After all, you are a busy business owner who has a full list of clients, aren't you? ... at least that's the impression you need to give.

Rants over ... for now.

So, where should your contact details be?

Don't hide them on your contact page. Your phone number and email address should be on every page, preferably at the top right or left hand corner. If you can include your contact details into the website header, fantastic.

And remember to include your contact details (or a link at the very least) at the point of making a sale. Don't leave it for your potential client to click away if they have a question.

**Your website home page – how important is it any more?**

It's you, the consumer, who drives today's web world; it's no longer ruled by the corporates. Today, everyone is able to have their say and control over what content they want to consume on the Internet. The biggest example of this change is the massive growth in video sites, especially YouTube. Just look at the infamous Justin Bieber; an overnight success because of the huge number of visitors he got to his videos singing in his bedroom.

As you start to embrace social media, you start to lose control over how and where potential clients come to click through to your website.

Your website home page used to be THE page to get right on your website. It was the entrance, the grand opening and the doorway to how your business was portrayed on the web. I know I have advised many clients over the years about how to create a home page that converts, engages and turns website visitors into potential customers.

But how many of your website visitors now come via this front door?

Several years ago, before I started using sites such as Twitter and Facebook, more than 55% of visitors came via my home page. Over recent years, that figure has dropped to below 32%.

My blog became incorporated into my main site in Spring 2009. Over the past few years, Twitter and Facebook have been fuelling my blog articles. In one month, one year my website statistics showed 31 different landing pages (the first page a website visitor is logged as visiting). In the exact same month, one year later, this figure increased to 134.

Now, I know that some of you reading this will have not started a blog yet, and you will have plenty to read and action from the next step in this book. You may have only just started to dip your toe in the social media waters, so yes – your home page may well still be that main front door where people find you.

But when you start to embrace and turn up the volume of your web marketing and social media, you will have to start thinking about the many doors to your website. And every page on your website needs to be prepared for your new visitors.

Here's what you need to do to ensure every page on your website is a home page:

**Opt-in offer in your static margin.** We will going in to much detail about opt-in offers in Step Five but it's important you think about this now when reviewing your current website. By having your navigation across the top of your website, you can make room for a static left or right hand margin to offer your newsletter, opt-in report or whatever it is you use to build your subscriber list. This static margin is automatically added to all new pages, which means you don't have to worry about remembering to add it.

Consistency and constant placement of your offerings will encourage familiarity with your website visitor and increase your opt-in conversions.

**Quality copywriting on every page**. Don't lose steam and write throwaway copy on pages you don't think people will end up visiting. For example, the "About Us" page is often the one page that many business owners just end up bunging on an address and a phone number. Often left to the end and put together in a hurry because you want your site to go live and you've had enough of all the to-ing and fro-ing. But if your name is mentioned on this page, then it's probably this page that will come up on a Google search for your name. Check it now – Google your name or your business name and see what "About Us" page appears on the list.

**Make every page count**. Don't create pages for the sake of creating content. The same goes for your blog articles. Posting poor quality, "cheap" articles and optimised pages stuffed full of keywords just to keep the search engines happy because you think that's what's needed to get your website high up on the search listing, is a waste of time. (Often these types of pages will actually work against you because if Google thinks you are trying to cheat the system and produce content just to get found, they may will penalise you and drop your site down its rankings for those key words.)

You will soon be the loser when the potential clients who find this content, click away because the content is dross.

**Contact details less than one click away**. Remember, if you make it difficult for potential clients to speak to a human being, you are going to lose business.

**Will your website ever be finished?**

Getting a website built is often something that sits on your to-do-list, waiting to be ticked off. You spend a few sessions with a web designer, write your copy and get it published. Tah-Dah. It's live. Your website is complete.

Actually your website work has only just begun. A website is NOT something that just gets ticked off from your marketing list. A website is an evolving tool which needs to be nurtured, cared for and grown to keep up with your business.

One of my clients was getting very frustrated with her new website the other month. She had decided to set one up using one of the readily available website-in-a-box companies. You basically sign up for a small monthly fee and you get a standard template, five pages to add what content you want and the ability to tweak colours and headers to suit your branding.

But after a week of playing around with different templates and writing copy for her 5 pages, she was pulling her hair out.

"Move away from the website!" I shouted at her. (And yes, I think I did shout because I couldn't believe she had spent so many hours faffing about with it.) It was time to take a break and stop trying to make it perfect.

My advice to her was to leave her website alone for a week and then come back to it for an hour every week over the next month or so. No more, no less. The site was working, the right pages were up, people where able to book a place on the workshop she was launching – but to keep fiddling to make it perfect before "launching" was just driving her nuts.

You see, a website should never be finished. When you run your own business, you are probably evolving and growing at a rate of knots. You start working with clients you hadn't thought possible, you create products and partnerships you hadn't quite planned for. You are being flexible to meet the needs and demands of your clients (or you should be.)

And your website has to reflect this. It's not a corporate brochure that once printed, has to be thrown out when out of date. It's a moving and evolving marketing tool that you need to be reviewing at least once a month.

If you decide to use a blogging platform such as WordPress, this will give you the ability to add features on over time. WordPress uses applications called plugins, which are like accessories you add to an outfit. WordPress gives the basic coding and structure of a website and there are literally thousands upon thousands of plugins – usually free – that you can add to your website depending on what features you may want to add.

For example, if you know you want to create a membership area to your website or you may not be ready for blogging yet, but in about three months you will, there will be plugins you can find and add with a couple of clicks that can transform your basic website into the marketing machine you want it to become.

If this gives you the confidence to get a basic website up and running right now, great. Don't try to build the full bells-and-whistles and make the project bigger than it need to be. Build it over time and you will get it done quicker.

## But wait ... what about search engine optimisation?

As this book is all about how to create the right web marketing systems to enable you to be successful in using social media, this is one topic that is best left to another time. We are focusing here on how to use the web marketing tools and engage with the right people in order to be successful in building your business. Your website needs to be found easily when searching on the likes of Google, but this is a topic for another book.

SEO is also an area that I see many business owners get scared into spending money on. If you were setting up an insurance company or selling baby clothes on the web, then SEO may well need to come up further on your agenda.

But for most of you reading this book, as coaches, trainers and consultants, SEO can often lead you on a wild goose chase. Trying to work out the optimum key word searches that someone may be using to try to find what you do can take up too much of your precious time at this stage. Investing in Google AdWords – pay-per-click adverts – may be a faster and more cost effective way of getting found on the internet.

To be honest, if you end up using a blog platform, such as WordPress, to create your site and follow the suggestions throughout this section and the next one on blogging, you will probably find your search engine optimisation happens naturally.

You are focusing on engaging and communicating with your target clients, so you will be naturally using the key words that your target clients will be using to find you. And a blog is a natural search engine optimisation caffeine machine, but more about that in the next step.

SEO is not a topic to be forgotten or brushed over; just left for another day and another book.

**Where next?**

Before you make final decisions on your website, it is really important that you read the following steps about creating a blog and opt-in offers. You WILL want to include both these aspects in to your design and strategy.

On to Step Three – giving your clients plenty of value.

## Giving your clients something to value

Some of you may be thinking "Oh Gawd, I don't want to set up and write a blog. I haven't got time for any of that." Others of you may be worried about having something else to add to their growing to-do-list.

I certainly don't want you feeling any pressure to set up and start blogging, as blogs are not critical to the success of all small businesses. But, when set up right, they sure do help your cause, especially when you are using social media to build your business and attract more clients.

Plus once you've got your blog established and have worked hard at getting a good following, you are able to slow down on the number of blog posts you create. Although, most business owners I know who get the blogging bug, find it hard to stop once they get going.

## Strawberries and cream

Blogs and social media go together like strawberries and cream. One without the other is OK, but together they make a perfect combination. Their tastes infuse and a simple dish of strawberries becomes a treat that you enjoy consuming, rather than just eat on the run if fancy a quick snack.

Social media can and does work without a blog. But your blog is the cream to the strawberries; it turns your social media profiles and updates into treats that your friends and followers value and spend time over.

And, more importantly to your marketing results, your blog will be the predominant reason why your friends and followers will visit your website; which I hope you are beginning to realise is critical to your social media success.

## OK, what actually is a blog?

A blog is a website that allows you to publish stuff (articles, videos, audio recordings) on the web instantly. A blog can be your website (because a blog is a website) or it can be a standalone site that works alongside your traditional static website.

If you are blogging already, great. I'm going to come on to how to supercharge your blog and make sure it is working the right way for your social media activity.

But first, for those of you who may still need a little convincing, here are the reasons why blogs work so well for small businesses.

## To blog or not to blog?

**Showcase you as an expert**: Being able to access the latest articles written by you (or someone in your team) will show potential clients that you know what you are talking about.

**Help people trust you**: If your potential client can get a feel for who you are and what you stand for, they will begin to trust you quicker. People buy from people they like and if your blog gives some of your personality, then it helps build that online relationship.

**Keeps your website fresh and alive**: Having regular updates makes your site looked loved and active. Plus search engines, such as Google, indexes websites more often when they are being updated. Google continually searches out new content to categorise and add to the search results it gives its searches; it wants to show the most relevant and up to date links to those searching. If you are providing new information for Google to index, it will keep coming back for more and rank you higher in its search results.

**Gives your target clients an opportunity to engage with you**: Blogs are designed for two-way conversations. You publish an article and then make it open for others to comment. It's your house, so you still have final control over what stays and what goes. If someone was to add inappropriate comments (swearing, liable, politically incorrect) then you can delete and remove.

However, I have to point out that this happens rarely; so don't let this fear put you off from using blogs to get known. Giving others this opportunity to agree, disagree and add their thoughts will make your blog come alive and spark conversations with potential clients.

**Makes you easier to share and spread around:** By having articles that give value, tips, advice or whatever goodness your clients get from reading them, you make yourself easier to get passed around to others. Articles can be re-tweeted, shared on Facebook, added to LinkedIn updates as well as re-published on other blogs. Because the article is a single web page, the dedicated url for each one makes it simple for others to spread the word about you.

If someone likes your article, they may want to tell their network about it. If someone in their network likes it too, the article may well get passed around their network as well. And so the sharing goes on.

People like to share good stuff, whether it's a funny cat video from YouTube, photos of their kids doing cute stuff or a well written, easy to read article that helps them with something in their lives. So the more your article can be shared around, the more likely you are to reach out to potential clients that you probably would have never had the opportunity of reaching out to at all.

Your articles can also be republished. And yes, this is a good thing. Copyrighting your stuff is obviously important, but that doesn't mean you want your article staying only on your site. I have several large, magazine style blogs with huge communities of readers who regularly re-post my articles and I get clients because of them.

Blogs are really a win, win situation. Making your clients feel good about you AND giving you that all-important Google juice to get you found on the internet. (Can you start to see now why I'm leaving search engine optimisation out of this book? If you have limited time and funds, focus on what your clients want to read about and your Google juice will start to happen without you trying.)

### Blog or Email Newsletter: Which one should you be doing?

We are covering email newsletters in the next step, but I felt it important to address this here in the blogging chapter. I get a lot of business owners ask me this question. It's as if they want to get things sorted as quickly as possible and by making the choice and making the decision to do just one, they feel it will help reduce their perceived workload.

You know what I am going to recommend, don't you? Yup, I think you need to do both. And these are the reasons why.

**Different delivery:** OK, this may sound obvious but it's a really important point to consider when thinking about how best communicating with your clients.

Blog articles are delivered via a website (your blog) and people can read your articles by either going to your website directly or reading your articles in a blog reader – think of it like an online magazine that you choose what articles you want to be given to read.

Email newsletters are delivered via email so are read in someone's inbox, along with all the other dozens, if not hundreds, of emails someone would receive each day.

Some of your clients will want to get emails. Some will hate getting emails but will still want to read your blogs online. Some will even subscribe to your blog to receive the latest articles by email. By making your articles available in both formats – web and email – it puts the choice in the hands of your clients. And you will reach more people if you give them this choice.

**Different subscription:** Blogs are subscribed to via the RSS feed – it's the little orange button with the white dots & lines in that you often see on a blog – whereas email newsletters are subscribed to by someone adding their name and email address to an opt-in box.

The big difference here is that you know exactly who has subscribed to your email newsletter as you have access to their email addresses. But your blog subscribers are anonymous – unless of course they subscribed via email.

The benefit to you of knowing these email addresses is that you can use your email list to proactively send out promotions and sales letters depending on what it is that you offer (balanced with quality of content, of course as you don't want to annoy your subscribers – but more of that later in this book)

The downside is that some people may not want to hand over such a private detail as their email address (for fear of being overly sold to, perhaps) and may prefer the anonymous nature of blog subscription. Again, different people will want to engage with you differently. If you only offer email subscription, which is of course more favourable to you, then you will miss out on people who prefer to watch, read and listen to you at a distance.

**Different platforms:** Your blog needs to be managed through a blogging platform such as WordPress. The content you write and publish is housed within this website, which you host and make accessible to people via the internet.

Your email newsletter needs to be managed through a newsletter management system. This newsletter system will manage your subscription list and enable you to deliver multiple email broadcasts simply and easily.

You can run and host your own email subscription service via your website. There are applications and bits of software that you can install, but I don't recommend this, which I explain in more detail in the next chapter. So, you will need two different tools to run both.

**Different purposes:** Typically a blog is used to showcase yourself as an expert allowing you to share your tips, advice and recommendations on topics that you specialise in. You may post 2 or 3 short articles a week and by regularly adding content, you are keeping a website active – which keeps Google very happy. A blog's purpose is usually the gateway to your business, inviting potential interested clients to take action: either leaving a comment, signing up for an email newsletter or even getting in touch with you directly.

An email newsletter is there to build up your database of interested clients. By collecting email addresses, this allows you to proactively communicate with your readers and possibly even send them back to your blog to give them more articles to read and hopefully comment on.

Your regular and consistent email communication will help to build familiarity and trust with your readers and it's from your emails that you will make your direct sales.

**Different readers:** Because of all of the above differences, you will find that you will also have different readers. Yes, some email newsletter subscribers will be avid readers of your blog, too. That's great. But most will only have the time and the inclination to do one or the other.

This leads me to coming back to the answer to the question: blogging or email newsletters - which one should you be doing?

Neither are mutually exclusive and actually work exceptionally well together. The same content can be delivered in both – no extra work needed there. And one can drive interest to the other – with the initial aim of increasing your subscribed database of email addresses of potentially interested clients and the ultimate aim of creating a successful long term relationship and turning readers into clients.

The answer should never be to decide on one or the other, as running both alongside each other works incredibly well.

---

**MAGPIE ALERT**

*Don't try to set up both a blog and an email newsletter at the same time. Start with one and spend a month or so getting that going before you embark on the other. Believe me, one of these projects is plenty to be doing at any time.*

---

### Hard work?

Blogs may sound like hard work. After all, if I was to tell you that it is recommended that you publish at least two or three articles every week to enable your blog to work effectively, you may well have fallen off your chair, clutching your chest as you have heart palpitations from the thought of all that writing to be done.

However, even if you just produced one article a week, that's fifty-two new pages of content added to your website. If you just published once a fortnight, that's still twenty-six articles to share on your social networks to encourage your target clients to check out your website.

Three articles a week is ideal (and if you really want to get your blog going, then go for one a day for thirty days – I promise you, it's worth the effort.) But if you can only manage three hundred words once a fortnight, then it's better than nothing. And it's certainly better than sending people to a static, brochure website that does not allow your target client to engage with you, read more about you and trust you that little bit more.

**Delegate or outsource**

If you really don't feel it's something you can do (or won't do) you do have the options of delegating this to someone in your team, for example an associate, or contract the work out to a virtual assistant or copywriter. There are also ghostwriters who can be found and hired.

There are also PLR (private label rights) websites that allow you to re-produce articles – for a small fee – under your own name. Yup, you can buy articles for a few pounds and publish them under your name as the author, completely legitimately.

If you do down this route, I would highly recommend you do take on a little editing and re-writing. You need to make sure it's your "voice" otherwise they will come across as fodder articles, not adding any value to your clients and helping them trust you enough to spend money with you.

OK, so I'm hoping you are ready to go for it. If blogging is going on the agenda, let's break this project down.

If you've got a blog up and running already, then use these steps to check where you are at with it.

You may find you need to re-visit some steps and go back before going forwards.

## How to get your blog up and running

**Decide on what your focus is going to be**: If you have done your market research right and written up your target client profile (see how important this first step is?) this shouldn't be a problem for you. Your blog articles should be helping your clients solve their problems.

Using one of the examples previously made in Step One; if you want to target women who have their second child and are concerned about the environment, then baby related, green issues are going to be right up their street. What sort of tips, resources and practical advice would they be interested in? Probably debates about disposable, re-usable nappies, baby food packaging and what the big supermarkets are doing to help them out. Plenty of controversial topics to get you noticed.

**Give your blog a personality**: What name can you give it? It may be something key word focused such as "Green Mums" or "Mums Who Care About the Environment." Or you could go down the curiosity route: "Throw Away Comments" or "Green with Envy."

By giving it a name, it will help with your marketing. It's far easier to email someone "have you read the latest on Green with Envy this week?" just as you would a daily newspaper or glossy mag.

**Decide on what platform to use**: There are lots of blogging platforms to look at. I've already been recommending WordPress, but you've got to be happy using it every day. Check out the resources page at the back for more options to look at. Each one will have its own merits, depending on your technical competence and personal preferences. Make this part of your discussion with your website designer if you are going down this route.

**Decide on the look and feel**: You may want to have your blog be your main website. You may prefer to have it painted and decorated so it feels as if it is part of the main house, but have more of "kitchen" feel about it, rather than the more corporate "drawing room" of your main website.

One of the reasons why I love WordPress is that it has the ability to add themes quickly and simply. With a few clicks, you can transform a standard, dull website into something professional and branded to your business. You can even have a different theme for your blog from your website; although I would heed caution to this as you don't want to confuse your clients unnecessarily.

**Plan your content:** Taking time to plan your articles for the first two or three months can take all the pressure off that "What do I write today?" feeling. You don't need much more detail than topic ideas and article headings. Mind mapping is a great technique to breaking down a big topic to enable you to come up with smaller three or four hundred word articles.

Each article should be easy to read in just a few minutes. You don't need war and peace every week, so keep your articles to between three and seven hundred words. Go back to the copy writing tips and recommendations, especially the point about bullet points. Using list type articles make it easier for people to read, but also easy to write and put together.

**Set and forget.** Another beauty of using blogging platforms is the ability to schedule blog posts in the future. If you prefer to spend one day in the month writing, simply add your articles into the blog dashboard and schedule a date in the future.

Your blog can be automatically publishing content whilst you are working on client projects, preparing proposals and even when you are lazing on a sun lounger whilst on holiday.

### How to get your blog writing started (or re-started if you've let it slip)

One of the downsides of writing is a blog, is … well, writing the blog. I love writing and I now find it easy to do. But there are weeks and sometimes months that I have struggled to discipline myself and sit down to write. I can't be creative all the time and I find it very difficult to write just because it says I have to in my diary.

Even when I know the benefits, get new clients from my articles and see an increase in my social networks and my sales every time I publish a new article, I still find it tough to keep it going week after week.

So I know how you may be feeling, faced with this mammoth task of creating content. If you have taken a break from your writing or you are starting from scratch, you may be finding it hard to get it going.

Your first blog post can feel daunting and, to be honest, a little intimidating. What will your first message be to the world? And who will be reading it? And there is nothing worse than a blank sheet of paper or screen to dull your creativity.

Here are some practical tips on how I have got my writing going and hope they may be useful to you if you find yourself in this dilemma.


**Print off a calendar for the month and give each day a topic.** For example, if you are a nutritionist ·· may want to have Monday as your detox day,

- Admin tips TOP P.A. → email management, diary management, expenses,
- Program tips – HOW TO – word, excel,

Tuesday as your veggie focus, Wednesday as your portion control day and so on. Giving each day a focus makes it easier to come up with article titles.

powerpoint presentation captivating etc,

**Article titles.** Once you have your daily topics, write down an article title in each of the days in your calendar. You don't have to write the article – just write down the title of the post.

You article titles could be in the form of a question, for example "What's the best way to start a detox?" "Help, I'm bored with nutloaf. What else can I make when the rest of my family is enjoying Roast Chicken?" or "Are smaller plates really the answer to portion control?"

Or it could be about tips and techniques, for example "The three things you have to know before you start any detox diet" "Five top vegetarian roast options, without having to resort to nutloaf" or "Portion Control: The number one mistake you will be making."

Once you've come up with the title, the writing should be easier because you've created an agenda. If the article ends up being bigger than you intended once you start to write, then break it down into two or three articles. They may even make a great three part series that you run over a week. Hey, you've now got a week covered in just one article. Easy.

Make a enbed documents,
- New App recommen. or website
- Blogs I love
- Training I have done
- Books I have read.
- Other VAs - blogs interviews of.

**Set aside a couple of hours of writing and schedule the week ahead.** Once you start writing, keep it going. Make full use of the scheduling function in your blog and time your posts to come out over the coming days. Once you get going, the writing becomes easier and easier. That first one is always the hardest so start tapping away on your keyboard now and watch the words flow out.

### The secret to creating great content

"What if people don't like what I write?"

"What if people disagree with what I write?"

Those gremlins in your head are very good at asking cutting questions like these just as you start to bare your soul and sit down to write your next blog article.

But it doesn't have to be this scary. Writing your articles needn't be tough at all. The secret to creating content is in the very word "creating." Where most small business owners go wrong is they think they have to "write" new content all the time.

The pressure of having to come up with something that is witty, insightful or even just plain practical can be just too much. So stop thinking about "writing" articles and start thinking in terms of "creating" them.

Here are my five top tips to creating content, rather than having to write it.

**Interview an expert in your field.** Rather than putting all the pressure on yourself, why not go out and find someone to interview. The fact that you are the one publishing the information will still make you the person or business that the reader turns to first when they need help.

**Check out your email sent folder**. Go through all your sent emails over the past week and look for one that you wrote to a client. Did you answer a question for them or provide them with a few top tips? If one client asked you for this info, then your subscribers would probably be interested too. Turn this email into a useful article for others to read.

**Review a book or product**. Your blog readers and social networks may be interested in the latest tools, books or gadgets. Showcase your expertise and give your opinion. If you are a photographer, can you recommend some photo sharing sites? If you are an image consultant, are there some new books out on Amazon? If you are a business coach, can you review some training courses or programmes?

**Create a recommended list of resources**. A great way of giving value to your readers is to put together a list of recommended websites or resources. Give your reasons why and show your readers why you are an expert in what you do.

**Writing differently from your website copy.**

You've already had some copywriting tips from me in the previous step. Although these are useful to your blog writing, writing articles needs different styles and approaches than the home page of your website, for example.

**Writing for your website.** The copy you write for your website should be selling what it is that you offer. Whether it's a product, programme, workshop or your opt-in report, your website copy sells it.

Just because you may have unlimited space and pages, doesn't mean you can ramble on aimlessly. Strong headlines are essential. Use questions to stop your online visitor in their tracks quickly (you've got less than a second to make an impact, remember.) And sharp, clear benefit-driven copy to outline how it is you may be the answer to your potential client's problems.

**Writing for your blog.** Whilst your website is there to sell your business, your blog is there is to build relationships. You need to stop being in selling mode and focus on giving value, content and useful information.

Your blog is the place to showcase your expertise, to share tips and ideas with your readers and build up a useful resource for potential clients to come back to again and again.

As each of your articles are one of the many doorways to your business, so welcome your readers and invite them to check out what is inside, linking relevant pages to your website where the selling can take place. If you try to sell hard at the doorstep, your potential client won't think about crossing the threshold.

Your language can be a lot more colloquial, too. There's no excuse for poor spelling and grammar, but don't get anal about it. So what if there is a typo from time to time in your blog article. Remember, completion, not perfection.

**The worst thing you can do when your blogging has lapsed**

Constant and consistent marketing is tough, especially when it comes to writing articles. But the worst thing you can do when your blogging or newsletters have lapsed is apologise for it when you have finally taken your pen to paper (or fingers to keyboard.)

I see it time and time again. A blog article that starts off with "Hi, it's been a while. So sorry, it's just that business is so busy I've just not had the time to write a new blog post/newsletter. But it's OK – I'm back."

Never draw attention to the fact that you just haven't made the time to blog or send out emails. Never highlight the fact that you, quite frankly, haven't been able to prioritise this all important, value added part of your business.

For those readers and subscribers who have missed you, they will be delighted to hear from you again. But for those who haven't missed you, they will only realise that they haven't actually missed out on your articles and content. And they may well be slightly peeved off that you haven't made the time to do this already.  Now, where's that unsubscribe link?

And once you've apologised and told your readers and subscribers that you're back ... then you've set yourself up for a fall if you lapse once again.

No, never apologise; just get on and do it.  Don't draw attention to your failings, no matter how guilty you feel.

JFDI.


**Where next?**

Blogging is not going to be right for all of you. As I mentioned at the start of this chapter, it is not a critical piece of the jigsaw puzzle.

However, if you haven't started blogging yet, I would like you to seriously consider how you may be able to incorporate a blog in your web tech marketing strategy somewhere down the line. It will really give a reason for your social networks to talk about you more and increase your chances of success.

Now on to Step Four – Your List. And this is NOT something up for negotiation. It is critical that you do this.

# STEP FOUR
# YOUR LIST

## Starting your engine room

Having a welcoming front door and plenty of interesting stuff for people to have a look at when they come to your website and blog from your social media activity is great ... but how do you turn those interested visitors into potential clients?

Unless you are selling classic retail products direct on your website – baby clothes, handbags, camera cases - you are going to find it incredibly difficult to sell your services, programmes and products – ebooks, audio downloads, membership sites – cold to your website visitors. I've already been planting the seed and telling you the importance of capturing email addresses over the first few steps.

Unless your potential clients have come highly recommended by someone, they are going to need to build trust with you. Just think back to the last few times you've got your credit card out and spent money via a website or picked up the phone to speak to a potential supplier. Surely you only spent money with someone once you felt they were a trustworthy business. If you were at all unsure about spending money with them, you would have moved on and found someone else, wouldn't you?

Creating engaging content and conversation with your network via social media is absolutely going to help start that trust. But having an online relationship with someone in social networks such as Facebook, where everyone is making small talk and chatting about what they plan to do at the weekends, is one thing. Arriving at a web page where you are offering a service and product for them to buy is another. You still need to nurture that relationship and make them feel comfortable in spending money with you.

### Asking your target client for a date

Let's think of your online relationships as dating. If a guy or a gal comes on too strong on the first date and you are not ready for their advances, the relationship is not going to go anywhere, is it? It may take a few dates before you trust them enough through your front door and invite them for coffee. And certainly a few more dates before you are ready to introduce them to your parents (and by then, it's probably a done deal – this is the one.)

If you go in hard on your website with lots of "BUY NOW" or "Just 3 hours left before they've all gone" approach, and your new visitor is still wanting to learn more about you, you run the danger of scaring them off too early.

So, what to do?

This is where your email marketing strategy comes in. You need to start up your engine room and find a way of encouraging your website visitors to part with their email addresses so that you can start building a relationship with them. I call this your engine room, because it's the oomph your marketing needs to be successful.

Here's how I got into email marketing when I first started up in business.

I started my first email newsletter in about month four of starting up my business. I had realised quickly that traditional marketing methods that I thought might have worked for me, were just not going to get the business in the way I wanted it. I wanted to have a business that gave me work nine months of the year whilst my children were at school, but generated income constantly and consistently throughout the year.

When I looked around at other coaches, they were all starting to offer email newsletters. It's fairly commonplace now, which is why you need to offer more than just a newsletter to convince potential clients you are worth sharing an email address with, but more of that in the next step when I write about your free offers. But back in 2005, it was all still quite new.

I started with fifty friends and family and set up an account with Constant Contact. I stumbled around for months but, slowly and surely, I started to figure out what I should be doing. I focused all my marketing efforts on getting people to sign up to my newsletter list. That is all I "sold" when I went out networking, spoke at conferences and events and it's all I offered on the home page of my website.

When I decided to run some workshops, I tentatively asked my email list if they were interested. And, guess what … I got bookings. Over the coming years, I was able to market and fill workshops every six weeks, which also filled my coaching practice.

My subscriber list is the MOST important business asset I will own. And it should be yours, too. It enables me to create, launch and sell products, programmes and services without the need of expensive advertising. It was the single reason why my Web Tech Club membership site took off the way it did. I couldn't believe how interested people were and how many signed up so quickly. It was because of my subscribers that I have worked so hard in getting and keeping.

## Marketing through the Perfect Storm

Your list will also help carry you through thick and thin, because we all have crap days. Sometimes whole crap weeks.

Have you ever been in this situation? You've typed out your marketing plan. It may even be stuck up on your wall or scrawled across a NoBo board. You're feeling very pleased with yourself that you have committed to some daily and weekly actions to ensure you are chipping away at generating potential leads for future business.

But then...

A client project goes wrong – you have to spend an extra ten hours on it because the client has changed their brief. Your laptop switches off. No warning. It's got to go to the shop to be fixed and you won't see it again for at least four days. Your child care plans go out of the window. Your au pair has hurt her back and she can't come to you for the next few weeks. And your mother, who is always on standby for you, is away on holiday.

Then, your partner gets ill. You have to run around organising doctor's appointments and picking up prescriptions. And to finish your whole week off, you get hit from behind when you are waiting at the traffic lights. You are OK but the car needs some serious garage work.

## The Perfect Storm.

No amount of planning or mental preparation can help you avoid this. Your contingency plans just can't cope with this amount of chaos and you have to focus on the here and now.

What's happened to your marketing plan? It's disappeared under the pile of post-stick notes, garage receipts and client notes. That's OK for a week or two. It's easy to catch up. But what if your au pair doesn't make it back to work and you have to start the whole child care planning again? What if your partner gets seriously ill? What if something else and then something else and then something else happens?

Ignore your marketing plan for more than a few weeks and your business is going to start to suffer. And this is another reason why you just have to focus your marketing efforts on building a database; a list of potentially interested clients who may want to spend money with you at some point in the future.

I'm not talking about the proposals you've sent out. Or the consultations you have had. Or even the database that you've bought to send out that promotional offer. I'm talking about the people who aren't ready to pick up the phone to you but are interested in what you do.

By offering interested people the opportunity to subscribe or opt-in for something on your website so that they can receive information that is valuable to them, gives you the opportunity to stay in touch with them over time. This is what is called "permission based marketing." Your target client has made a decision to add their name and email address into an opt-in form on your website and by doing so, expressly gives you permission to send them emails.

The more you can automate this process, the more effective and efficient your marketing will be, especially when you are in the middle of the Perfect Storm.

My Perfect Storm lasted about six months. My dad died of Lymphoma almost three years ago. Before then, we had an eighteen month roller coaster period with three lots of chemo. My business had to move a peg or two down. I still ran some events and still worked with a few clients, but during the summer of 2009, I basically "shut down" for about six months. I put my proposed marketing club on hold (which turned out to be a good thing because it morphed into the Web Tech Club) and spent that time driving up and down the A303 from Hindhead to Devon most weekends, being a mum during the week and a daughter at the weekends.

When I came back to work in the autumn of 2009, I thought it would be a hard slog to build my business back up. But it actually wasn't as hard as I imagined. My email newsletters and blog had carried on periodically. I was able to continue with writing articles and schedule stuff to go out. And it was this constant drip feed of valuable info that allowed me to pick back up again and ride out that Perfect Storm.

I'm sharing this very personal story with you to help you make sure you plan for that Perfect Storm. Make sure, before you start flying off into the social media world and start collecting your shiny objects, that your marketing plan includes some form of email newsletter or opt-in offer via your website so you can build up a database.

If you do make time to create an email marketing system, you'll find it far easier to pick up from where you left it if – and when - you hit that Perfect Storm.

OK, have I convinced you that you have to get your engine room sorted? Great, let's get moving. But first, let me share with you the common pitfalls that most small business owners fall in to. The more you know what to avoid, the more effective your email marketing systems will be.


**The five most common email marketing pitfalls and how to avoid them**

How many email newsletters have you signed up to over the years? Whether it's a free report you've asked for or to get the latest news, it's become the norm for many businesses to be capturing those all-important email addresses.

But how many of those email newsletters that you've signed up to have been any good? How many have added any real value to your day? And how many have been nothing more than clutter and spam in your inbox?

When an email marketing system works, it can transform your business and enable you to grow quicker and faster than you ever imagined. But when done badly, your emails can be causing your potential clients problems.

And problems are not what you want to be offering, are they?

These are the five most complained about problems that emails can cause and I bet you have found yourself cursing over one or more of them yourself. So, go through this list first before we get stuck into how you get started with your email marketing system.

**Get added without being asked**. Top of the Pops and coming in at Number One is my favourite email gripe - business card dumping and website mining. There are still plenty of business owners out there who feel it's acceptable to upload lists or manually add email addresses to their email marketing system, without having asked permission from the person.

Email marketing gets the best results when it's permission-based. Don't be lazy. Work out a real reason why someone would want to receive emails from you and offer your emails as an opt-in service only.

**Can't read them**. As more of us are using smart phones and tablets to read and send emails, our screens are getting smaller and smaller. Fancy, graphic based newsletters may look great on a 13" screen, but when squashed into an iPhone it just makes you want to hit that delete key.

Your subscribers may prefer text-based emails, too. Images can work well for designed based businesses, but if certain email servers block certain graphics, you're left with pretty ugly emails that may not be able to be read.

Personally I do a mix. A "pretty" but simple template built in HTML (the language used to create web pages so you can create images and design) newsletter with graphic headers and images to help draw attention to the articles and offer. And text based emails for promotions or "quick questions" that I use for market research and help with creating and selling products.

If you do want to use a HTML template, keep your newsletter design simple. Keep it to one column and avoid those magazine styles, unless you've done your research and found out that this style actually works for your business.

**Too many**. You must have come across this one. You've signed up for a free report and before you know it, you've had four emails in the first 24 hours … three of which have been recommending (selling) affiliate products. Wooooh there, horsey!

Yes, you can't be shy about selling your business. You've got to make your offers to your subscribers because you are not a free publishing house (are you?) But watch your scheduling, especially at when you are busy promoting your latest product or event.

You may find you have to spend some time and emails to build up the trust from your subscribers. Give some value before you go for the sale – make friends first – and you'll find you won't need to go heavy and "make the sale". You are not a hormone-induced teenager trying to score on their first date.

**Too few**. On the opposite end of the scale is not receiving enough. A lack of consistency will dilute your efforts and will only make your subscribers wonder who you are. They may well have forgotten who you are if they signed up for something over a month ago before getting any follow up.

In fact, I got an email from such a business this morning. It must have been at least two months since I had heard from them last and yet they were obviously gearing up for a promotion. Hmmm.

Be in touch with your subscribers regularly – at least once a fortnight if you are serious about marketing your business. Little and often goes a very long way. Lots of business owners talk about offering a monthly newsletter, but that means just twelve emails a year. That's simply not enough if you are serious about developing relationships with your subscribers.

**Can't unsubscribe easily**. Grrrrr. Another common problem that really shouldn't be here if businesses used proper email marketing systems. Replying back to an email with "unsubscribe" in the subject heading really is a pain. And as for having to re-submit your email address once you click through to a web page ... well, talk about having to jump through hoops.

Once your subscribers have had enough of you, make it easy for them to leave. A "one-click" unsubscribe button is offered by all the major newsletters systems, so there is really no excuse for not being able to offer this. You don't want your subscriber clicking that "spam" button do you?

## What email marketing system to use

I've mentioned already the importance of subscribing to a "proper" email marketing system. Yes, this will mean spending money, but most are cheaper than you think. Do not EVER attempt to run an email marketing system on the cheap. And never EVER run one via your outlook or email server.

Prepare for success. You may be able to cope with manually adding one or two new subscribers a week to your system, but what happens when you have a couple of dozen? What happens when you get up to hundreds? You need to subscribe to an official email marketing system that will give you automatic opt-in and opt-out processes, as well as the ability to send mass emails out without the internet service providers thinking you are a spammer.

 When someone adds their name and email into the opt-in box on your website, you want these details to be automatically added to your database and a welcome email to be sent.

 You may just need a basic newsletter system – something that sends out a nicely formatted newsletter to your subscribers once or twice a month. Check out the resources page for recommended websites to look at.

If you are planning on selling events, products or programmes via your website, you will need an autoresponder system bolted on. Autoresponders are automatic emails that are sent out when someone buys or subscribes to something on your website. They really are the most brilliant bit of web tech kit you will want in your business. Once you start using them, you will wonder how on earth you managed without them. Again, check out the resources page for recommended websites.

The final consideration on which system to go for is whether you will need a shopping cart system. This will give you ability to offer discount coupons, affiliate programmes and a more efficient system for tracking past and current clients. This may take you into more complicated email marketing systems with more features than you may need, so it is worth deciding how fast or slow you want to grow over the next year.

138

**MAGPIE ALERT**

*Choosing the right email marketing system can send you into a real spin. It's really easy to spend days and weeks discovering new systems and avoid making the decision which one to go for.*

*I would highly recommend you first decide which category you fit in to: newsletter, newsletter + autoresponder or full monty shopping cart. Then find up to three (and no more than three) websites to review and test out. Give yourself a deadline when you propose to finish the reviews and make a decision.*

*You won't find the holy grail. No email marketing system is going to tick every single box that you have. It's impossible and I know because I'm now on my third email marketing system in eight years. Start with a system that you will enjoy using and if you grow out of the email marketing system you've chosen over the next year or so, you can change and transfer your list.*

### Keep it simple

Just set up what you need to get you going to start with. Whatever system you decide to manage your email marketing on, is best grown over the coming months and years. Your priority is to focus on getting your initial subscriber sign up set up. If you are offering workshops or programmes and doing these manually (for example, "send me a cheque and I'll send you a confirmation") keep it this way for now.

This email marketing project will explode otherwise and you'll lose your way. You need a sign-up form for first time visitors to get going with your web marketing systems. Do this first and come back to the rest (setting up your ebook sales, workshop confirmations) as time allows you.

**Is the set up all down to you to do?**

Even if you consider yourself to be technically competent, I promise you that there will be times that you will feel like pulling your hair whilst trying to set up some of these email marketing systems. I have threatened to throw my laptop out of the window on numerous occasions whilst trying to work out what code goes where and making sure the right people get the right emails in the right order.

But you may be relieved to know that not all the technical set up is always down to you. As you are reading this book so that you can understand what needs setting up, you may be wondering why I am telling you this now.

What is the point of learning more about these web marketing systems if you don't have to be the one to do it?

It's because it is important that you understand the strategy behind all the set up. There is delegation … and there is dumping. You can only delegate successfully if you understand what and why certain systems need setting up. If you decide that you haven't got time to understand how all this web stuff works and just want to find someone who can take it off your hands, you may end up with something you didn't ask for.

It's why so many business owners end up with websites, for example, that don't work effectively for them and yet they end up with huge invoices to pay because they decided to leave it all in the hands of an expert. The website may be technically brilliant and beautifully designed, but as a marketing tool it stinks because the expert wasn't clear on what your business objectives were and how you wanted to convert your visitors to clients.

The website designers, marketing assistants and administrators that you end up hiring may be good at their jobs but very few offer the high level marketing strategy that you need to be in control of. And, to be honest, very few actually realise what is needed to make social media marketing successful. There are too many who still floundering in the dark, trying to work it out for themselves, let alone be an expert for you.

So going back to my point about how it doesn't have to be all about you getting all this stuff done. You won't be able to do a lot of the tech set up that you are reading about in this book; nor should you feel any pressure to learn the technical ins and outs.

This is where virtual assistants (VAs) can massively speed up the set up process for you; technical administrators who you hire on an hour-by-hour basis.

If you want to get started on finding a VA to help you get started with your email marketing systems right now, you will find plenty of tips and suggestions about how to go about recruiting a VA in Step Seven.

## Where to put your email opt-in forms

The most "eye-balled" part on your website will either be top left or top right corner and this is the place that your opt-in form needs to be in. The most effective place for your opt-in form is probably going to the top right hand corner, making sure it is "above the fold." It is worth testing this over time and comparing your opt-in results against different positions. But to start with, go for this top right hand corner spot.

This phrase "above the fold" goes back to classic newspaper advertising where the premium spots were above the folded part, at the top near the headlines. People are more likely to spot the advert at the top, than at the bottom. It's the same principle online; you don't want potential subscribers to have to scroll down to find it.

Your top right corner sign-up form also needs to appear on every single page. This is why it's best to incorporate it into your design template of your site so it never gets forgotten.

I would also recommend you add an opt-in form at the bottom of your home page, depending on your content and style of website. If someone has taken the time to read and scroll down your home page, make it easy for them to sign up right there, rather than expect them to scroll back up and find it.

Plus add an opt-in box at the end of each blog article. You can do this as the author link – just like an email signature – or if you are using WordPress for your blogging platform, there are plenty of plugins to find and use to help you add this automatically. If someone likes your article, then there is every chance they may want to opt-in to receive further articles direct to their inbox.

You most certainly want to have a dedicated website page, also known as a squeeze page (more about these in the next step) that only offers visitors the option to sign up. This will allow you to have a dedicated url to send interested people to whilst you are out networking or wish to add in a follow up email.

For example www.yourbusinessname.com/giveaway. You could also set up a dedicated domain name as mentioned in Step Two.


**What about pop-ups?**

Pop-ups have to be the single most annoying thing on the internet (well, for me anyway.) But it has been proved time and time again that pop-ups do work and having one that appears once someone has been on your site for a couple of minutes can help encourage more people to sign up to your offer.

I have one on my main website and every time I sigh and scratch my head about whether it's the right thing to do, I look at how it has increased my subscriber rates. So, it stays … although I do carefully set it up so that it doesn't pop-up as soon as someone lands on my website, as well as have it set so that it doesn't appear for that person for at least another 30 days.

If they increase your subscriber rates, do it. If they reduce them, check your pop-up settings to maximise its effectiveness. And if that still doesn't do anything to attract more subscribers, then stop.

What will work for some, won't work for others.


## Double Opt-ins

The systems recommended in the resources page are almost all North American based companies. Thus they offer the North American double opt-in practice that adheres to the CAN-SPAM act of 2003. Double opt-in is not a legal requirement in the UK, but I believe it's still best practice to offer it.

Yes, having your list set up as double opt-in means you can't upload a spreadsheet full of email addresses into your email marketing system. But isn't that a good thing? It is far more effective having 100 people read and act on your emails than have 10,000 people ignore and report you for spam?

So what is double opt-in? It is the process of confirming a subscription. Rather than just adding a name and email into an opt-in box and receiving whatever was on offer, the person would receive an email instructing them to click on a link to confirm their email address first.

Initially it seems to add an added complication to the process. So why offer it?

Let's check out the downsides of double opt-in first:

Confirmation emails may not get through – if it gets stuck in the person's spam filter, they won't be able to confirm.

If they can't confirm, they won't receive what it is they have requested and you won't be able to email them any future promotions or newsletters.

It takes effort – OK, it's only one click but for people who are not used to a double opt-in process they may not bother, especially if they are using their phones to check emails.

Confirmation emails may delay the process – sometimes it can take a couple of hours for an email to get through because of busy servers. If you are offering instant access … it may not be. There is every chance that a percentage of people who sign up for whatever it is you offer on your website will not confirm their subscription. And what a waste of a new subscriber.

Or perhaps not. Here are the upsides to using double opt-in:

Serious subscribers – would you prefer one thousand freebie hunters on your list that may not ever end up spending a penny with you or one hundred potentially interested clients who will? The more effort it takes to receive something free, the more likely the person is to act on the information being sent to them.

Clean database – if someone adds a typo or wrong email addresses, they won't receive the opt-in request and thus the email won't be added to your mailing list which will keep your bounce rates low (the number of emails that don't arrive at their destination.)

Prevents mistaken identities – think of this process as a safety check to stop people adding their friends email addresses without their permission.

Double opt-in is usually only once, depending on which email marketing system you choose. If you offer further reports or downloads, your subscriber will only need to confirm their email address once.

The decision to offer double opt-in is for you to make. I prefer the double opt-in option and I offer it to my newsletter subscribers. But it is not an essential part of the process.

### The secret to creating great content for your email newsletter

Go back to the step on blogging. There are some really great tips and suggestions on how to get your creative juices flowing and writing great articles. And yes, the articles you write for your blog can be exactly the same articles that you send out to your email subscribers.

## What else do you add to your newsletters?

I send out a fairly typical style of newsletter that many other successful coaches, trainers and consultants use. I start with an introduction - usually very personal, mentioning something about my week. I make an offer – you absolutely have to make an offer otherwise what is the point of sending out an email newsletter. These are business generating marketing tools and when you sandwich these promotions and offers with great content, it works.

The lead article comes next. And yes, it is just the one article. Occasionally I will run a "best of" and run three or four of the top rated articles in previous months, but that is usually during holiday times when I want to get one up and running quickly.

I then finish off with a list of "Recommended Resources," usually sending people to targeted pages on my website or affiliate links of products that I use.

If you want to see at first hand what I send out and how I use a mix of autoresponders and newsletters, go to www.CanDoCanBe.com/newsletter and sign up for yourself.

My biggest tip is to always link your email newsletter article to your current promotion. If you are running a special promotion this month or offering a new workshop, write around one of the challenges that you know your clients have before using that product or service. Not only will it provide interesting and useful reading, it will help your subscribers take action on what it is you are offering.

### Does size really matter?

Everyone seems to be focused on numbers, don't they? How many followers can you get on Twitter? How many friends can you collect on Facebook? How big is your network on LinkedIn?

How big does your mailing list need to be before you can make any sales?

Numbers, numbers, numbers.

It seems that everywhere you look, everyone is obsessed by size of lists, so does the size of your mailing list really matter?

There is no doubt that the bigger your mailing list is, the more likely you are to make sales. After all, if you trying to sell twenty places on a workshop to a database of fifty people, the chance of you filling all twenty places is minimal. Even if everyone on your database is interested in the topic, they may be on holiday, have a meeting that day or just couldn't justify the expense at that particular time. Therefore, the more people you have, the easier it is to market your events, products and programmes.

But all this focus on numbers can be demoralising, stressful and not a lot of fun when you struggle to get just one or two newsletter opt-ins every week. You certainly don't want to be desperately tweeting away ten times a day, asking your followers to click through to your newsletter opt-in page.

Here's the good news. The quality of those you attract to your mailing list is what matters most. That phrase "size doesn't matter, it's what you do with it that counts" rings true for your mailing lists.

Putting more focus on attracting quality sign-ups will mean that what you do with your mailing list – whether that's selling e-books, workshop programmes or one to one services – will work far more effectively for you.

So what are some of the rules when it comes to successful list building strategies?

**Know your target client.** The more focused you are on the exact client you want to work with, the easier it will be to attract them.

**Know the pains and worries of your target client.** The more you know about what the problems your clients have, the easier it will be to come up with a great give-away to encourage them to part with their email addresses.

**Offer results, rather than the solutions.** Your target client isn't really that concerned about how you go about helping them. They just want results. So a "Monthly Newsletter" which is rather blah blah, suddenly becomes desirable when it becomes "The Five biggest mistakes that small business owners make – and how you can avoid them." Same opt-in process – just presented in a different way.

We are going to go into a lot more detail on these offers in the next step. They are important.

**Be personal.** If you are sending someone an email, try and make your introduction as personal as you can. You don't need to be sharing the full details of your personal life but make yourself more human and your subscribers will think of you more as a friend who is emailing them, rather than a business entity.

It's why I often recommend adding a photo of you somewhere in your newsletters too. If people can see who your emails are coming from, they are going to form a deeper connection with them when they see them appear in their inboxes, which in turn increases your open rates (the number of subscribers who actually click your email and view it, as opposed to deleting straight away.)

**Be clear on the language your clients use.** Tone of phrase, images, how you address someone, specific jargon – all of this matters. Write and present yourself in a way that relates to your target client.

Yup, you've guessed it. There's a theme going on here with all these tools, isn't there? Doing your groundwork on your target client profile really does pay off and I'm not going to apologies for repeating myself again and again because I know I may have to say it a few more times for it to sink in with some of you.

## What next?

Setting up your engine room can be a BIG project, so it's really important that you do make sure you have the right support in place, hence why I recommend hiring a VA to help you.

Give yourself the space to plan out your timelines and project actions. This is not something that you can set up from scratch on a rainy afternoon.

Whilst your email marketing system is being set up –which can take a matter of days, weeks or months depending on the time you can make available to this project – you will need to take some time to consider what the fuel will be for your engine room.

On to Step Five – creating your free offers.

# STEP FIVE
# YOUR FREE OFFER

## Giving your clients something to love

Although a regular email newsletter is integral to building those relationships with your target clients, offering it as your only means of subscribing to your list is no longer unique or special enough. You can't just hope that the words "Free Newsletter" will entice someone to sign up to receive your emails.

Your clients are being bombarded with messages left, right and centre. It doesn't matter what you buy any more, everything seems to come automatically with an email newsletter ... although what most businesses call newsletters end up being endless sales messages and up sell offers. So when your target client sees a newsletter advertised – even if it's free – they will hardly be tripping over themselves to sign up.

As consumers, we no longer need to receive marketing messages from companies to enable us to make a decision to buy something. We have all the information we need right within Google, our social networks and our real life friends.

If you want to buy a new car, for example, your first step would probably be looking at what your friends are driving. You go ask them what they think of XYZ model and what they like/dislike about it. Your next move may be to go to your social networks and ask your online friends. You may post a question and see what response you get. And then, the third step is probably heading over to Google and typing in the model name along with words such as "review."

Why would you need to receive a newsletter from car manufacturers or garages to help you make your decision? You don't want to get sold to and you will probably get the answers you want from the three steps you've made already.

So your "Free Newsletter" – unless it's come highly recommended from a friend or colleague – is just not enough to motivate your target client to part with their email address.

You've got to give them something they will love to get their hands on.

### What's in it for them?

Why would your target client make a decision to click to your website and decide there and then to part with their email address? What's going to stop them in their tracks and make them ask themselves "Oh, I want that"? What's in it for them?

"Free" may be an obvious starting point. But just because something is free, doesn't always mean that you want it, does it? "What's the catch?" your website visitors may be thinking. "There's no such thing as a free lunch."

On the other side of the coin, you don't want a whole load of freebie hunters either. People who sign up for free stuff usually don't take the time to read, listen or act on what it is you are offering when they've actually received whatever it is you've sent them.

Go on - check out your hard drive right now? How many e-books, special reports and audio recordings are sitting there, unread and untouched? I know I have probably dozens, if not hundreds of free files that I have collected over the years just waiting for me to act on them.

You not only want potential clients to sign up for something. You want them to consume it too. You want them to listen, read and act on the advice, tips or help that you are offering in your free offer. Building your list is one thing, but if you aren't engaging with that list and the people who are on the list aren't engaging back, it just becomes a numbers game. And that game gets very demoralizing when you find very few people from your list actually buy from you.

What would you prefer to have? A list of 20,000 emails and you struggle to sell not even half your twenty tickets to your next workshop or seminar? Or a list of 1,000 and having a waiting list of people who didn't get the opportunity to get their hands on one of those twenty tickets which sold out within two weeks?

Yup, I go with quality over quantity any time of the week.

Before we dig a little deeper into understanding what your target clients will get excited about, let's have a look at the various ways you can deliver your offer. There are a number of different formats you can use. Whilst most of them are digital, do take note of my suggestions on creating a physical product.

EBook – a basic PDF is the simplest way to start. Create something up in a Word document, convert it into a PDF (most Word programmes will allow you to "save as" the document as a PDF right there and then) and ta-dah. You have a file that can be delivered, opened and read on any PC, Mac, internet browser and email server. It's a safe file as it can't contain any viruses that a Word document could contain, which means that your target clients won't be receiving any extra unwelcome goodies with your offer.

Kindle version – although PDF's are the easiest and simplest documents to create, take a moment to think about the ways your target clients are reading stuff online today. A PDF can be read in a Kindle, but not as easily as a Kindle document itself. It doesn't take that much effort to convert the file, especially if this is outsourced, and be offered as a link direct to the Amazon Kindle site to be downloaded once someone has shared their email address with you.

PowerPoint Show – this isn't going to be the right format for many of you but if your target client uses PowerPoint slides day in, day out in their working day, this could be something to consider. There are several online PowerPoint sharing sites, including SlideShare.net, which is by far the most popular and is used regularly in the business community particularly because of its association with LinkedIn.

Audio – mp3 recordings that people can download and listen to either on their smart phones or in the car are perfect for clients who like to listen. You are also engaging at a higher level than just passive reading. They are going to hear your voice, your tone of phrase and decide whether you are the right person to do business with. Services such as AudioBoo and Soundcloud allow you to upload files and embed audio clips in blog posts, Facebook and Twitter.

Video – taking the level of engagement further, seeing and hearing you is really going to ramp up your relationship with this new potential client. A one-off video or online course could be delivered through a course of autoresponders and links to video sharing platforms such as YouTube and Vimeo.

But what about physical products? Digitally delivered products are obviously cheaper, and in most cases, free to deliver. But if you are serious about building a list, then there will be some of you who will need to consider a physical product that your target clients can actually touch, feel and hold.

There are two main benefits to you by offering a physical product. The first is you get to ask for their postal address, which will mean you can start engaging with them via direct mail, postcards and letters in the future ... not just by email. Secondly, your level of engagement goes up a notch. Because most businesses offer digital products as their free introductory offer, we rarely get stuff through the post anymore. So when your target clients get an envelope in the post, there is something "wow" about it.

You do have to consider the costs. Offering physical products may become part of stage two in your marketing strategy, for example. Start small with a digital version, test to make sure it's something that your target clients want and then turn it into a physical product when you are ready to take it up a notch.

On the other hand, if you really have to stand out because you are in a fiercely competitive market place, then this may be one marketing activity that is worth the investment to get started on straight away. If you know what your average client spend is, you can work out what you are prepared to spend for each new client lead.

For example, if your average client spend is £3,000, then spending £5 for each new client lead could be money well spent. Do your sums rather than automatically reject these ideas because of the cost implications.

What physical products can you send out to your target client?

Printed reports – If you don't want to risk having to order 1,000 copies and then be tripping over boxes every time you walk in to your office, then consider print-on-demand. There are a number of fulfilment houses and print-on-demand companies who can provide quotes on how much a printed report would be for each individual order.

Choose a fulfilment house or print-on-demand company that can link automatically with your opt-in email marketing system. This will enable an order to be sent to them each time someone subscribes to your opt-in form, saving hours of manual ordering.

CDs – instead of giving someone a download link, send the CD in a nice CD case in the post. Again, a fulfilment house or print-to-demand companies can do these, meaning you don't spend an hour each day posting and packaging.

DVD – if you have a video course, the same applies. Instead of a CD, create a DVD to go out. Again, print-on-demand.

Print-on-demand will obviously push the cost of each individual product up. You will pay for the convenience of having just one product printed and produced at a time. It may also delay the time it takes for someone to receive it, but not more than a day or two.

However, this increased cost per product may be far more favourable than having those boxes cluttering up your office as well as reducing the amount of initial investment needed to get started.

Start small and if proving popular and the right thing to do, invest in a few hundred or thousand to bring your overall costs down.


## Solving problems

But … before you get carried away with the technical aspect of what it is you offer and taking back all these lovely new shiny tools to your nest, you need to make sure that what you offer is going to be of incredible value to your potential subscribers.

The more "wow" you can create, the better.

Going back to Step one again, you can see why knowing your target clients is essential in all of this planning. If you've done your homework and spent the time on your client profile, then this should be a fairly straightforward exercise. (I'm like a broken record, aren't I?)

You need to know exactly what problems your target clients have – what keeps them up at night, what brings them out with a cold sweat on a Monday morning, what niggles away at them all weekend making them irritable with their family – and create a solution that you can deliver in a way that is useful, interesting and worth sharing.

Let me give you some examples:

**If you were a weight loss coach** – rather than offer a free newsletter on how to diet, can you create a product around "How to lose weight without going anywhere near a gym" or "The secret diet that allows you to still eat chocolate."

**If you were a website designer** – rather than offer a free monthly news update, can you create a product around "The five mistakes almost all businesses make with their website … and how you can avoid them" or "Three steps to getting your website live in less than two weeks."

**If you were a virtual assistant** – rather than offer the latest tips and articles, can you create a product around "The Number One tool that will manage your diary better and enable you to have every Friday off" or "The secret short-cuts to incredible presentations that win you a new client every time."

Whether each of these products is created as a PDF, mp3 download or DVD that arrives in the post is up to the expectations and usability of your target clients. You need to make some decisions and get on with it.

But there is one thing that is THE single one thing that will make or break your free offer success. And I'm pretty sure you are probably starting to guess what it is going to be from the examples above.

## It's all in the headline

Your clients are not going to be really bothered about the way you deliver your free offer. I know, I know – it sounds like I'm contradicting myself here after what I've shared about delivering products. The delivery style creates the "wow" factor. But it's the cherry on the cake that sells it.

The cake is good. Oh, yes. But when you walk into a patisserie and are faced with a plethora of pastries, cakes, doughnuts and tarts, it's the toppings, chocolate swirls and cherries that catch your eye, isn't it?

When there are lots of cakes to choose from, make sure your cherry stands out. And your cherry that sells the cake, is the headline. I see this a lot, especially with coaches and consultants who aren't very technically able, but get carried away getting good at their new tech toys. (Yet another symptom of the Magpie Syndrome.)

Let me give you an example. It's based on a true story of one my clients ... but all facts have been changed to protect the innocent.

David has set himself up as a career coach. He's good and has already made a reputation for himself. He's decided to ramp up his marketing this year and he's going to maximise his opportunities within LinkedIn. He's decided to create a series of videos to help people with their CVs. He's found out from his clients that one of the number one problems they get stuck on when they started to decide to look for a change in careers is what to do with their CV. Great – he's done his research and he's pretty confident that he's on to a winner.

The target clients he is looking to attract respond really well to videos and, as he wants to use one of the fastest growing mediums in today's market place to help promote himself, he wants to give it a go. He gets himself a flip camera, buys Camtasia and sets about recording a six part video series about getting a CV right.

David is the first to admit he's not the most technically minded. He's never done anything like this before but he's finding the whole process fascinating. He's learning all sorts of new stuff about video making and he's even signed up for a six week course to teach him more about YouTube marketing.

He's doing all the editing himself. He's up to midnight most nights for at least two weeks, playing around with sub-titles and captions, but he's beginning to feel like a bit of a guru on the whole video creation process.

Finally, after three weeks of hard graft, he's done. He sets about putting together a squeeze page (more of that in a moment) and launches it to the world. The video on the squeeze page goes into a lot of detail about the fantastic videos and how easy it is to watch and learn. After all, David is proud of his production.

What happened? It was a bit of flop to be honest. It's a well put together video course – absolutely. But the title of the course was "How to write your CV". Not the most compelling offer in the world, is it?

The good news is that it didn't take much tweaking to that title to make it the success that it deserved. And David changed his introduction video on the squeeze page to focus more about the content, rather than the delivery and production. It's the classic "selling features, not benefits" mistake that David made.

The cake is important, but you need the cherries to sell in a busy, time deprived society, which is exactly where most of your target clients live now.

## Cheese is good

OK, so my food analogies may be going a little awry as cheese and cherries don't go terribly well on cakes. But bear with me and allow me to switch over to savoury now. You'll notice that my previous product suggestions for the diet coach, website designer and virtual assistant all had very cheesy titles.

Some of you may have even shuddered at the tabloid-ness of a couple of them. That's OK. You do need to adapt phrases and words to suit your style and your target clients' turn of phrase.

But as the title of your free giveaway is the single most critical success factor, you won't go too wrong basing the structure of your headlines on how one particular industry lives and dies by their headline success.

## Women's Weeklies, Celeb Mags and yes, even The Sun

For the very best headline inspirations, I highly recommend you hop down to your nearest newsagent and buy up a selection of the weekly women and celeb mags on offer. Even reach over for today's copy of The Sun. These tabloid newspapers and magazines have to sell tens of thousands of copies each and every day and week. They rely on the front page headlines to shift these copies.

You may not be into sharing "Five Celeb Secret Diet Tricks" or "The Number One reason why Daniel Craig would date you" but you can certainly use the ork of the headline. Substitute the words " "diet" "Daniel Craig" and "date you" with hat make sense to your clients and both these headlines could probably work for your free offer.

"Five Secret Money Making Tricks" or "The Personal Trainers' Secret Perfect Abs Trick."

"The Number One reason why sales teams miss their monthly targets" or "The Number One reason why Alan Sugar would hire you."

Go on, try it. Get a copy of The Sun and convert today's headline to suit the problem of your target client. It's a great starting point to give you the top selling headlines for your free offer.

## One size does not fit all

OK, so this next section may push you over the edge. I've given you stacks of ideas on how to go about creating a free offer to entice your target clients on to your list and now I am going to suggest that you may need more than one.

I know, that's more work to do.

But seriously, if you want to really see results from your social media activity, you may find that you will need to develop different free offers to attract different people – even if they are the same target client.

One person may love getting a report that they can read on their Kindle. But someone else hates reading. The only way they like to learn new stuff is by listening to their iPod whilst at the gym. And someone else, who likes the sound of that free audio download, doesn't actually take action and share their contact details with you until you offer a free DVD in the post.

All these people fit your target client profile ... but they all consume information in different ways.

The same goes for the headline and topic. Going back to the diet coach example I used for headline suggestions – one target client may jump at the chance to find out how they can lose weight without going to the gym; they absolutely hate gyms. But someone else actually likes gyms and they don't understand why their weekly weights routine is having no impact on their muffin roll.

This doesn't mean you have to go into a whirlwind of free offer creation for the next month. No, no, no. But what this does mean is that you need to be continually coming up with new ways and free offers to keep your list building fresh.

For example, it may be that every three months, you need to review your free offers and create something new. It could be that you set yourself a target of every six months. It's a marathon not a race. Your business does not have to be an overnight success ... because, frankly, most overnight successes have taken several years of hard grafting before that happens.

What I want you to think about is making your free offers a long term strategy - not as a tick-that-off-my-to-do-list and ready to move on for something new.

Here's what I have on offer at the moment. First of all, I have to admit that I do stray from my rules a touch by having a free newsletter on offer on the home page on my main website,

CanDoCanBe.com. I have worked hard to build a loyal following with a credible reputation so many people do seek out my newsletter because they've heard good things about it. If I were starting out in today's marketplace offering what I do, it just wouldn't work, as I would be an unknown. The motivation to sign up to unknown's newsletter is just high up on most people's agenda any more.

But I do offer specific free offers depending on which website or page you end up on. For example, I also currently have a "Copywriting secrets for business owners who can't write" report. This is a collection of articles I've written over the years and is offered on a pop-up when you visit my blog.

There's also a "free pudding" to be had over at my Web Tech Club where you can get a free taster training session to get a feel for what the club is all about and decide whether it's the right thing for you.

And finally, I have my infamous "Twitter Checklist for Business Owners" which has to be my longest standing, free offer success. I put this together more than two years ago and it is still my number one list builder; which considering I haven't done anything or tweaked anything on it for months and months, is pretty good business building activity as far as I am concerned.

I've also run lots of one-off list building promotions, from live teleseminars to offering free downloads for a limited time only; each one being a different topic that has reached out to different people within my target client profile over the years.

So, don't create just the one front door to your home. Work on creating lots and lots of front doors over the next few months and years and watch your social media success go up and up.

### Squeeze Pages

I've made a couple of references to squeeze pages already and this is as good as any place to talk about them in more detail. For those of you who don't know what a squeeze page, it's a web page that only offers one call to action, usually an opt-in for a free offer. It basically gives just the two options to the visitor: opt-in or leave. It squeezes that email out of the person.

I've also been known to use the phrase "one banana website," especially when you may be selling on that page, rather than just an opt-in offer. You don't want to sell the whole bunch of bananas to your client and confuse them over what they should be doing. You just want to sell them the one. Choice is bad for you, so if you take away the choice, the decision becomes easier.

Squeeze pages can be on your main website, so there's no need to think about having a new website built for each new squeeze page. It doesn't become part of your site navigation so it can't be found unless someone clicks on the specific url for that page. Plus, you take off the site navigation when someone views that particular page so that the person can't navigate anywhere else away from that offer. They can only opt-in or leave.

You can either hire a website designer or web tech VA to create these sorts of pages for your website. If you use, or plan to use, WordPress for your website, this design process becomes incredibly simple as very little in the way of complicated script writing is needed. There are even free and paid-for plugins that allow you to create these yourself. (See the resources pages for recommendations.)

The link for these squeeze pages can either be an extension of your main site, for example www.yoursite.com/4stepstosuccess; or you could buy a specific domain and have this re-directed to the page as described in a previous chapter, for example www.4stepstosuccess.com

Either works; it just depends on the length of the url (too long and you risk urls being broken or misspelled if someone is free typing, rather than clicking through) and how else you may be using this free offer in the rest of your marketing.

Are squeeze pages critical to the success of your free offer? In a word, no. And if you are just starting out on creating your social media presence, creating your website or beginning your email marketing, then you may find that you have plenty to get on with over the coming weeks, rather than faffing about and getting your head around squeeze pages, too.

I am giving you permission to take things one step at a time here. As I've said already, you aren't in a race and you run a real danger of getting the "rabbit caught in headlamps" look if you try to do everything all at the same time. "Analysis Paralysis" is another phrase I love to use with some of my clients.

But if you already have your website up and running and you've got an email marketing system working for you, then squeeze pages could be a great project to getting going to increase the impact of your free offers.

## Size doesn't matter - it's all in the follow up

Whenever you read the latest article about list building from some marketing "guru" or internet marketer, they always seem to follow the same theme: "It's all in the list."

Hopefully you have realised during this book that if you aren't building a list of potentially interested clients, then your social media marketing activity could be pretty much a waste of your time and money. Building a list IS important. Critical, even. But the phrase "It's all in the list" is simply not true.

A list of names and email addresses will not create the success of having a constant and consistent steam of clients, banging on your door to spend money with you. It's how you engage with them once they are on your list that matters.

## It's all in the follow up.

Relationship marketing is a phrase that gets banded about a lot now. We've gone from "direct advertising" marketing in the 80's and 90's when most companies would spend their marketing budgets shouting about their messages to us, all of the time. The only way to get your business back then was to shout the loudest and most consistently, which meant lots of advertising and stuff through the post.

As the internet began to give us, the consumer, the opportunity to research our product buying more carefully, rather than just rely on the information that businesses thrust in our faces, the power has shifted from companies to the consumers.

Over the past ten years, companies have started to think more carefully about their marketing and the more savvy ones moved from the "direct advertising" marketing to developing relationships with their customers. Relationship marketing was born and it's what a lot of companies think they are doing well at.

The truth of it all is that most companies, who think they are doing relationship marketing well, are actually sucking at it. They got clever at building a list, yes. But all that meant is the relationship they have with their customers is that they are now shouting at them, using their first name and sending their messages directly into their inboxes and phones.

OK, I'm having another one of my rants again. But this is where so many small businesses get it so wrong. They focus on building a list and when they get to their first thousand emails, they rejoice because they think they are building a relationship with them.

They send out emails with special offers and latest news on products and programmes and rejoice as their list grows and grows and grows. Their free offers attract new potential clients every day and they think they've cracked it.

The truth is that this kind of relationship marketing is almost as bad as the old fashioned "direct advertising" marketing of the 80's and 90's. They may have slashed their advertising budgets but how much do the people on their list really care about what they do and what they offer?

The focus on your marketing should not be about relationships; it's got to be about engagement.

Engagement is a two way communication and having permission to send out emails to someone is just the first step in the right direction. The big leaps will start to happen when you begin to have that two way conversation with the people on your list.

You send them an email and you get replies back.

You publish an article on your blog and you get comments back.

You post an article on your Facebook Page wall and you get shares, likes and comments back.

You send them a customer survey and you get responses back.

Your engagement can again go several big leaps forward when you start to reply back to their replies, comment back to their comments and thank them for their responses.

That's true engagement; when your list feels a connection with you and what you offer and they are having a two way conversation with you.

Now, not all these people on your list who are having this two way conversation with you will become paying clients. But that's OK. Because they will feel a connection with you and what you offer, you can bet your bottom dollar that they will be talking favourably about you to their family, friends and colleagues.

You marketing starts to reach out to potential clients that you would have never thought of connecting with and all because of your level of engagement.

Coming back to your follow up; if your focus has to be about engagement, rather than a one way, personalised "shout" what do you do once someone has opted-in to one of your free offers? You just don't have to time to email everyone personally every time they opt-in for your free offer. The last thing you want happening is getting dragged down by emails all day.

## The beauty of autoresponders

I've already mentioned autoresponders in the previous chapter on your engine room and email marketing systems. And this is when the sheer beauty and brilliance of autoresponders magically impacts your marketing.

Autoresponders are simply automatic emails that are sent out once someone has opted-in and been added to a list. You can set emails to be sent out at fixed intervals for the coming days, weeks and even years.

But be careful of falling into the trap of shouting, rather than engaging. Most small business owners who embrace autoresponders make the same mistake over and over again. They think they are relationship building, but what they are actually doing is sending out personalized sales messages with the sole purpose to get someone to spend money with them.

Now I am not suggesting you shouldn't be selling. Of course, you are in business and if you don't make a clear offer, most people just won't think of spending money with you. But very few small business owners think about how to use their autoresponders to engage.

Here's an example of an email that arrived in my inbox just a few hours before me writing this chapter:

> "Hi Karen. I just wanted to say that I think yours is the best example of the use of autoresponders. They really do feel as if they are personal and always relevant, with a point about my business rather than yours."

I get a lot of emails like this. I'm not sharing this to show off and brag. I just want you to understand that once you start to use autoresponders, you have to think about your target client's needs … and not yours.

I could write a whole book on how to write effective autoresponders - which is actually quite a good idea, so watch out for future titles from me - but to get you started, here are some tips.

**Write to one person, not a crowd.** The more personal you can get and write on a one-to-one basis, the more the person will feel you have written and sent that email to them, and them alone. Think "Dear John" style, without actually wanting to break up with them.

**Ask questions about them.** A great way to start with your first email in the autoresponder series is to ask your subscriber a question such as "What are you most frustrated about?" or "What's your biggest challenge about XXX?"

I do this with almost all my free offer autoresponder series and although the majority of people do not answer, the ones who do I can almost guarantee 9 out of 10 of them will spend money with me within the next six months. This is because I always try my best to reply to each one personally, which helps take that impersonal list building marketing strategy into engagement mode.

**Sandwich offers with valuable content.** Once they've signed up to your free offer, don't assume that they are ready to buy everything you send them. You've shared something great with them, now share more great stuff. Keep repeating the value over and over again as you want to make sure you are right there at the right time when they are ready to buy. Some people may take months, maybe even years, so don't write a six week follow up ... plan for six months or more.

---

**MAGPIE ALERT**

*Remember, you can write those six months of autoresponders over the coming months. You don't need to have written six months of autoresponder emails before you launch your free offer. Get the first three or four done, and then schedule in the rest to keep you with your first few subscribers. This will stop you trying to be perfect and focus your efforts on getting the job done and your social media marketing working for you.*

---

**Write in stories.** If you preach to your new subscribers in every email, your subscribers are going get a little fed up. Preaching doesn't engage, but stories do. The more you write about case studies, client success stories and bring characters to life, the more interesting your emails will be to read. Starting this book with the story about Rebecca was no accident.

Hopefully this chapter has inspired you to create value and help you become shiny shiny attractive to your target clients. Free email newsletters are a great step in the right direction, but avoid becoming blah blah mediocre. Creating free offers – including the content, product delivery and set up – is hard work, but you don't have to do this all by yourself. You may work for yourself and run your own business, but that doesn't mean you have to be the one to do everything, all of the time.

Make sure you read the final chapter in this book as it demonstrates how to use other people's skills and experiences to get you to where you want to be going quicker. But first, the sixth and last step to your social media marketing success – your social media.

# STEP SIX
## YOUR SOCIAL MEDIA

As I explained in the introduction about how to read this book and get the most out of it, this is not a step-by-step manual that will show what buttons to press when. This particularly applies to this chapter on setting up your social media.

Sites, particularly the likes of Facebook, will change, take away and add new features constantly. Just when you think you know what goes where, they go and change the admin settings or take away the feature. It's a common problem that I am sure many of you have experienced already in this new shiny world of marketing.

What this book is all about, and particularly this chapter, is to take you up above the detail and help you think, plan and act on creating a social media system to attract the right clients to you constantly and consistently throughout the year.

I will be answering the question of which social network first? I will help you decide which one is going to work best for you because you don't have to set up a Facebook Page just because everyone else seems to be doing it. This is not about helping you create a marketing plan based on what everyone else is doing. It's about helping you come up with a marketing plan that will work specifically for you, your business and your clients.

I will also be sharing ideas on what content to share, how much to automate the process, reminding you to check your privacy settings, showing you what to do when you get the negative comments, as well teach you to delegate as much of the technical stuff as possible.

There are hundreds, if not thousands, of social media sites out there in hyperspace. There will be some niche ones that you will need to seek out depending on your target client profile. I couldn't possibly cover each one in detail. I would be writing for months and then have to update it all again because they've all changed in the time I've been writing.

However, I will be focusing on the four big players as these will be the four social networks that most of you reading this will be interested in and will end up using on a regular basis: Twitter, Facebook, LinkedIn and YouTube.

Many of the examples used during each section of this chapter – such as content and privacy settings – can be applied to any four of these networks. So do keep asking yourself how different points could be applied to different social networks that you end up using.

There are also geo-tagging social networks out there. These are networks that allow you to "check in" to certain places based on your location that your smart phone has you registered at. Every smart phone has a built in sat-nav and in the same way you may use your map applications to help you find your way, this same technology can tag you to a particular location in a particular network. (Don't worry – these features can be switched off and I cover this in the privacy settings section.)

If I was writing a book aimed at retailers, this would be definitely an area I would be covering in detail. There are many high street shops exploring these geo-tagging tools and offering discounts for a number of visits. Just like a loyalty card, instead of getting a stamp on your "buy five get the next free" card, your smart phone checks you into a central network.

However, this book is aimed at coaches, trainers and consultants and although geo-tagging sites such as Foursquare are interesting if you attend conferences and travel a lot, for most of you these sites will just end up being another shiny toy for you to bring back to your nest.

When I cover niche sites and forums later on, there may well be some of you who will find geo-tagging sites useful to look at so don't ignore them if your target clients or key contacts who you network with are using them.

### Reasons why your social media marketing won't work

Before we start diving into how to get your social media marketing working with the rest of your web marketing, it's worth taking a quick look at the reasons why your social media won't be working.

Some of you will not have dabbled yet, I'm sure. The shiny toys won't have tempted you. But, the lure of the shiny new world of marketing has captured many of you and I am pretty sure that many of you related to that story of Rebecca at the start of this book.

Facebook and Twitter have to win the prizes for being the two biggest knee-jerk social media sites out there. Because many of you probably started to use Facebook for true social sharing and signed up because your "real-life" friends and family were on there, it's easy to start dabbling with a Facebook Page and try using it to promote your business.

Twitter, on the other hand, makes it so simple to set up a new account that it's hard to believe that all you need is a name, email address and password and Bam! ... you can tweet to the world.

However, when you do set up your Facebook Page or Twitter account, it's easy to wonder what all the fuss is all about. It doesn't become the holy marketing grail that you had hoped it would be. It hasn't made a slightest bit of difference to your bottom line.

If you worked your way through the previous five steps, you will have probably worked out what you are doing wrong already and be deciding what actions to take to start getting it to work. But, if you've come straight to the back of this book and decided you wanted to skip through all the hard work of getting your website, blog and email marketing working first, here's the problems you will – and may be already – encountering.

**No target audience.** This is THE biggest mistake that small business owners make with all marketing activities. As I've explained throughout this book, it's not just a social media mistake. If you don't take the time to identify exactly who you want to reach out to, then you may as well stand on your local street corner and hand out leaflets to every passerby. One day, someone may be interested ... but that's an awful lot of leaflets.

**No objectives.** Again, not just a social media mistake, if you don't know what you want to achieve, how will you know whether you have been successful or what actions need taking each and every week. If you haven't taken the time to decide what results you want, don't bother setting up a social networking profile in the first place. It will be a waste of your time.

**Lack of content planning.** There's nothing worse than starting the week and avoiding your new shiny Facebook Page because you haven't got a clue what to post on your wall. It is a drain on you, both financially and emotionally.

**No personalisation.** How personal you get does depend on your business brand. But hiding behind your corporate logo is just not going to work on social media for a business like yours. You don't necessarily have to use a photo of you on your social networks (although I do recommend that you do) but you do have to be "you" when using social media.

Sharing really private stuff is not necessary either, but there will be some public private stuff that will make you human. See later in this step for more on this topic.

**Chasing numbers and pleading for more fans.**
Numbers do make you feel good. It's great to be loved by hundreds of people, isn't it? But numbers don't always guarantee success. It's the engagement you get with those fans that will build trust with your brand and ultimately help turn them into paying clients. And nothing looks more desperate than regular tweets and posts asking and asking and asking. Create great content and you naturally attract the right people to you.

**It's all about you.** Even though you have to be "you" on your social networks, that doesn't mean you become a business bore. Sharing stuff about your business and making special offers all the time is boring at best, spammy at worst. You've got to ask yourself "What's in it for my network?" Share stuff that interests your fans – trade secrets, useful resources, funny videos, latest industry developments and sneak peeks of new products. Much more on this later.

**Automated feeds.** Automating one or two things to be posted on to your social updates is OK, but be careful of making all your status updates automated. Again, this topic is covered in more detail later in this chapter.

**No marketing systems behind your social media activity.** And the last, but quite possibly the most frequent mistake made, is if you don't have the right marketing systems working for you - taking interested people from your social networks into your website(s), on to your mailing lists and building relationships with them in your own home – then you run the risk of being a popular, but very poor person.

Take the time to go through each of the five steps outlined before this one on social media. If you ensure you know who it is you want to engage with, have a website, blog and email marketing systems set up with the right free offer(s) available, this will rocket fuel your social media success.

## Time to put out your welcome mats

Now that your house is in order and you are welcoming your new guests in and showing them around, whilst sharing valuable and interesting insights with them, it's time to get out there and start laying out your welcome mats. It's time to start inviting more people to the party.

## The welcome mat principles

Too many small business owners focus solely on having their conversations with potential new clients in their social networks, rather than in their own home. Being active on any social network is obviously important; you can't just set up a profile and wait for people to find you. Sharing content, tweeting, updating your status - it is what gets people to notice you and start to engage with you.

But concentrating all your efforts on the getting comments, shares, likes and re-tweets is not the way to grow your business. It's very important to be thinking how you can bring your online connections, friends and followers into your house. When they are in your house – your website – then you can start talking business with them.

Think of the classic door-to-door salesmen. They don't seem to exist where I live (much to my delight) but the few who do turn up, will never make a sale standing on my front door step. They use all their persuasion techniques to get invited in so they can get their presentation folders out and start the sell.

Now, before you start all that wincing and grimacing at the thought of selling, I am not suggesting you go for the hard sell as soon as they cross your threshold. No, no, no. This is where your engine room – your email marketing system – comes in.

## Offer them your welcome gift

As with any new houseguest, you offer to take their coat. Ask them if they want a drink. You make them feel welcome. You may show them around your house (direct them to different pages on your website.) But first and foremost, you make them feel welcome.

This is where you offer them your free gift; your report, online course, recorded interview - whatever you have decided will be of most value to your target client.

It's your way of saying thank you and it gets you on to first base, which is getting their name and email address. You aren't holding a gun to their heads. If your visitor says, "No, but thank you," then that's OK. You are not in the business of collecting any old email addresses. But what you do want are email addresses of people who are potentially interested in what you do.

## Not just your home page

During Steps Four and Five, I introduced landing pages, squeeze pages and using specific web addresses for your free offers. When you set up your online profile, you can add a specific website address.

Now, most business owners automatically add their home page. But with your engine room buzzing in the background and targeted free offers to offer on different social networks, you can send them to any page you like on your website.

Here some examples of what you can do on each of the four main social networks.

**Twitter:** You have just one website address to appear on your profile. Create a specific welcome page on your website for anyone who comes via Twitter. This can help keep the Twitter tone and style and avoids that jump from Twitter slang to a more conventional web page. On this page, offer a special welcome gift. If you can relate your offer around the theme of Twitter, all the better.

For example, I offer a Twitter Checklist on my Twitter welcome page, which, not surprisingly, goes down very well. Have a think about how you could focus your free offer around the Twitter network and whether this would work for your target client.

### MAGPIE ALERT

*Remember Rebecca at the start of the book. Be careful of showcasing your Twitter expertise if this doesn't help solve your target client profiles. It may be that you can offer a resource that lists the top twenty Twitter sites to follow or little bite-sized tips of 140 characters emailed every day.*

You can add a web link to your profile too, but as you only have 160 characters to introduce yourself, you haven't got the space. Avoid using url shorteners here just so you can decrease the length of your website address. Most people will be reluctant to click them unless they know you are an absolutely trustworthy profile. Too many spammers use them to direct people to phishing and virus sites.

**Facebook Page:** Rather than every person automatically seeing your wall when they first find your page, you have the option of setting your "default landing page" to any page you like. What this means is that you can create a specific landing page that only gets shown to people who haven't liked you yet. This allows you to have a page that encourages people to like your page, which a lot of businesses now do on Facebook. You have probably seen dozens of these already in your Facebook travels, but check out any of the big brands such as Red Bull, Pepsi and French Connection for examples.

However, you can take this one step further. A like is great, but what you are really after is their email address. You can use this landing page to provide an incentive and give your new fan the option of signing up for your free offer, thus getting those all important contact details.

If you want to see an example in action, just check out my own Facebook Page – www.Facebook.com/ Webtechclub. If you have liked it already (thank you) then simply unlike it, refresh the page and like it again.

You can create these bespoke landing pages fairly simply using any number of third party applications (see recommendations at the back in the resources page) however it is worth contracting this set up to someone who does this for a living. It's not expensive – anything from £50 to £200 depending on design time – and it will save you hours and hours of hair pulling.

---

**MAGPIE ALERT**

*Even if you consider yourself to be technically able, don't try to do these landing pages yourself. It will waste hours of your time learning what button to click when. If you don't have the cash flow to do this yet, then just stick to leaving your wall as the default landing page for now. It took me the best part of two years to get my landing page sorted. It's not critical but it certainly ups your game when you are ready to move forward with it.*

---

Once your landing page has been created, go to "Edit Settings" and in the "Manage Permissions" page, you can change the default landing page to the specific page that has been created.

**LinkedIn:** You have three website links on your profile, all of which you can edit and label the link to suit your needs. Most LinkedIn users will only make use of one of these and simply have a link that is called "website." Doesn't quite provide much of an incentive for someone to click through, does it?

Make full use of all three links. For example, why not have links called "Latest blog articles", "Secrets to XXX" or "How to XXX without XXX" and have the link sent through to the specific page on your website. If you use the headline of your free offer, this provides a much stronger incentive for someone to click through to your specific free offer page.

**YouTube:** If you plan to use video in your marketing, then having a YouTube channel is easy to set up. You have one website address showing on your profile so as with the previous social networks, can you direct people through to a targeted YouTube page on your website?

You also have the option of adding a web link with every video you upload. Every time you upload a video to your channel, you can add a description of what the video is all about to help people to decide whether it's worth viewing.

I recommend you start off each description with a website link that takes interested people to a page that allows them to sign up for more about what you are showing in the video. To make this link active, you do have to add the "http://" before the "www" as this will turn it into a hyperlink (a clickable link rather than just text that someone would have to copy and paste.)

So tweet away, comment and update your profiles, but remember you are still talking to them on your welcome mat. When people are interested enough to check out your profiles and click on your website links for more information, make sure you are taking them to a page which encourages them to take a step closer towards being a client.

### Can you tweet about your free offers?

Absolutely! You want to be sprinkling your tweets, wall posts and updates with the occasional mention of your free offers. Don't overdo the promo tweets though, as it will come across as shameless spam.

I will cover this topic of what content to share and how to do it without you having to be live on the networks all day later in this chapter.

### Which social networks should you set up?

The three musketeers of social networks are Twitter, Facebook and LinkedIn. They are often batched as a threesome and I can find myself saying Litter and TwinkedIn from time to time. But this doesn't necessarily mean that you set up all three automatically.

The fourth "big" social media platform is YouTube. Although this doesn't operate the same way as Twitter, Facebook and LinkedIn, in that you add daily updates and interactions, it is an incredibly powerful "back room" to showcase your videos. It is the place to upload any video presentations you may have as you can share links of these videos on any of your social profiles, as well as your own website and blog.

As more and more businesses are using YouTube, it is beginning to act more like a social network and if you look closely enough there is a very active online network going on there between active YouTubers. So do keep a close eye on this in coming months.

## Unloved and forgotten

The danger of having profiles set up on all the social media sites you can log into, is that it can become too much to keep them updated. An unloved and forgotten Facebook Page or Twitter account could actually do you more damage than having none at all.

If an interested potential client who loves Twitter hops on over to your account and then gets disappointed because the last tweet was more than six weeks ago (Yup, six weeks is a loooong time in the Twitterverse so be warned any of you with Twitter accounts dormant for six months or more) they are going to wonder what's happened to you.

Being busy with client projects you may well be, but your potential client may draw other conclusions – have you shut up shop? Have you gone on holiday? Do you not care about your clients?

At the very least, they probably won't choose to follow you and this may be the one way that this person prefers to connect with new suppliers and businesses they want to do business with.

## Which one first?

It is tempting to go about setting up every social networking profile going but as this often leaves you with a huge mountain to climb – and a mountain that you may not have needed to climb in the first place – a better question to ask is which one should you start with first? And the answer is going to be different for each you.

It's whichever social network is going to benefit your business the most.

If your clients are corporate based, then for goodness sake, get yourself sorted on LinkedIn. If your clients are part of the mummy market, then Facebook is your core focus. If you want to concentrate your efforts on raising your media presence, either in the national press or on the radio, then Twitter is a great place to hang out with journalists and editors.

I'm not saying that LinkedIn is only for corporate clients, Facebook only for the mummy market and Twitter is only for journalists, but if you've done your homework, figured out your target client profile and made sure you've taken Step One outlined in this report, then coming up with the right social networking site to start with is going to be easy for you. Certain social networks are going to be used more by specific target clients and you need to decide on who you want to engage with first and do your market research to find out which ones they do use.

It will save you months of wasted time and effort, faffing about on social networking sites that don't produce any results for you.

Oh and whilst I'm at it, you have my full permission not to set up certain accounts if your clients don't use them. It is not business critical that you have all – Twitter, Facebook, LinkedIn and YouTube – set up … contrary to popular belief. Just because everyone else seems to have an account set up in one particular social network, is not a valid reason for you to set one up.

Let's dive in and have a more detailed look at each of these four main social media sites.

## LinkedIn

Out of the four social networks mentioned above, LinkedIn is the one that most suited-and-booted business people feel comfortable with. It's professional and designed to be a business networking tool.

LinkedIn is like a business conference; it's like being at the local networking event or annual trade show. People turn up expecting to do business and, as everyone is there to do business too, it's feels OK to talk business.

What started out as a recruitment platform where people joined to be head hunted and look for new careers, LinkedIn has grown to be a global business community attracting small business owners right through to CEO's and Managing Directors.

LinkedIn is still very much a place where the head hunters hang out. Its paid-for subscription is designed to help people access the hundreds of thousands of people registered on the site. But for most of you reading this, the free account is plenty good enough for you to get started. By all means, check out the paid-for subscriptions but get the basics sorted first before you start spending any money.

### Why is LinkedIn such a powerful network?

**Professional and business like:** Your profile is based around a CV format and the groups and discussions that happen on LinkedIn are around business topics, rather than what you had for lunch that day. For this reason, even the most senior business people feel it is appropriate to have a profile on LinkedIn.

**Based on the six degrees of separation:** For those of you who haven't come across this theory, the six degrees of separation demonstrates that six people connect us all to each other. By searching for key people you want to contact, you can easily see if they are already connected to someone in your network. You can see how closely linked someone is to you by whether someone is 1$^{st}$, 2$^{nd}$ or 3$^{rd}$ degree.

If they are 1$^{st}$ degree, they are connected with you already. If they are 2$^{nd}$ degree, it makes this an easier connection to make if the person that connects you both can introduce you, rather than you go in cold.

As your network starts to grow on LinkedIn, the more interesting connections start to happen. For example, just check out the suggestions that LinkedIn make for you; it's amazing how certain people "pop" back into your life based on who you are already connected with via your LinkedIn network.

**LinkedIn Groups:** Start diving under the hood of LinkedIn and you find thousands of active groups and communities. If you are looking to go hang out with a particular target group of people, then LinkedIn probably has an active group of these people already. Search the groups by key words or names to help you find what you are looking for.

I wouldn't recommend you join as many groups as you can find. Be selective and join the ones that you feel you have the time, and the inclination, to contribute to. By all means, "lurk" to start with but you need to reach out and contribute first before you can start to get the two way engagement with your target clients.

And for goodness sake, don't spam a group with sales messages about your latest seminar or product. That's the easiest way to get yourself thrown out of a group and blocked by key people.

**LinkedIn Answers:** Similar to the groups feature, this section is hidden under the hood as well. There is a busy and engaging question and answer section; divided into specific categories, you can use these sections to ask questions yourself (particularly useful if you want technical questions answered) or, if you want to build your online profile, answer the questions yourself and start showcasing your expertise.

The person asking the question can vote for their favourite answer and, over time, you can get yourself known as a expert in your field via these votes.

**Google juice:** Because of the size of LinkedIn, this site is indexed regularly (registered and checked by search engines so that relevant web links appear in search listings.) If you want to get found online quickly and easily, a LinkedIn profile can be one of the quickest and most effective ways of doing this. References to you on your website may not be indexed fully because Google has not had time or reason to check you out. But a LinkedIn profile that has a well-connected network will have you top of your name search in no time.

### Top tips on getting started on LinkedIn

**Professional Headline:** At the top of your profile, you have what LinkedIn calls your Professional Headline. You have a limited number of characters to add here and this will appear next to your name in certain searches and news feed listings. Think of it as your answer to "So, what do you do?"

Many people stick with "Business Owner" or "Managing Director" and frankly, this is dull, dull, dull. You've got the opportunity to stand out in searches and make yourself look more interesting for people to check you out. So make this your

Headline that draws people to click on your profile, rather than job title.

**Your photo:** Professional, head shot please. This is not the place to be adding your holiday snap shot that has your other half's head chopped out and you holding up a glass of wine. People make snap judgements about what they see and your LinkedIn photo needs to sell you and your brand.

By all means have a more relaxed photo on Facebook, but LinkedIn is a business networking site so be business like in your photo as people may not take you seriously.

**Benefit driven profile – not a CV:** The challenge many business owners have with LinkedIn is its CV based profile. You are probably not using LinkedIn to find a job, but you do want people to stop and take notice of your profile when they view it.

Avoid listing a whole load of things that you have done over the past few years and focus on what's going to be of interest to your potential clients. Your clients aren't looking for an in depth career history but they are looking to see how you can help them solve their problems.

You also have the option to add and move the sections up and down your profile page. For example, your summary could appear at the top providing a good introduction to you and what you offer, and then you may move your recommendations or a Slideshare presentation up so that it appears above your work experience. This may provide a better way of showcasing what you can deliver, rather than the chronological list of past employers.

**Website Links:** As mentioned already, you have the option of adding three website links to your profile and, more importantly, you have the option to change the text of the link to something more engaging than "My Website."

What about adding a link to a specific page that outlines a number of successful case studies? What about sending people to an example of your work or portfolio? What about a specific offer you can make to contacts from LinkedIn? Your home page is OK, but you have the opportunity to use this real estate far more effectively.

**Status updates:** Once a week, update your status and tell your contacts what you are up to. Mention a new project you've started. Tell people about your new product launch or workshop. Share a link to an article on your website or blog. This is your opportunity to sow the seeds (rather than just brag and brag about your achievements and latest successes) and share what you do in a conversational way.

Note that I have mentioned once a week as a recommended starting point for updating your status. If you are going to be active on LinkedIn and use it as your primary social network, then once a day may be more appropriate and help with getting noticed and starting conversations with new contacts.

Your LinkedIn status update is not a tweet, though. Your LinkedIn network do not and will not want updates from you every ten or fifteen minutes, so get noticed but don't get noisey.

## Twitter

Twitter hits the headlines almost daily. With quotes from footballers' tweets who are in trouble (again), politicians saying the wrong thing or the latest trends (each season Xfactor creating thousands of tweets every second) it's easy to see why it's one of the most hyped social media platforms.

Twitter is like a cocktail party. Tweets (the 140 character status update published on Twitter) are pinging around left, right and centre in their thousands and, like all good parties, if you try to listen and participate to every conversation in the room, it's overwhelming. Reading every single tweet will only give you a headache.

Twitter is a dip in and dip out network. You can't be expected to read every single tweet from every single person you follow, every single day (and night) of the week. And nor should you want to; it's not email.

Ideally, you want to log in to your Twitter account once, twice or three times a day. When you do log in, scan through the latest tweets from the people you've followed, replying to your @ replies (public messages sent to you) and DMs (private messages sent to you) and add your own tweets and @ replies to others.

(OK – I know that last paragraph is going to sound like a foreign language to some of you. But I promise you, once you get past the perceived techno-babble, it all begins to make perfect sense. You've got to jump in and join the party to help you understand the rules and language.)

### Why is Twitter such a powerful communication tool?

**Quick and easy:** With only 140 characters to each tweet, you have no choice but to be concise. This is one of the reasons why I love Twitter so much; you can't spend long coming up with a verbose reply. Simple, short words work best.

**Access to information:** Whatever your profession or industry, there will be buckets of resources for you to access. Blogs, publications, directories, news channels; they all present you with a free and easy way of keeping your finger on the pulse. And fast. Breaking news stories can hit Twitter a good few hours before the national news channels have even checked their sources so if you want to keep up with the latest information in your sector, then find out who has their fingers on the pulse and follow them.

**Global reach:** Whichever country you want to do business in, Twitter can give you that doorway to open. You have the ability to search for key influencers and target clients from the location of their profiles, as well as their tweets; as many smart phone users are now GPS tracked, so are their tweets.

**Local reach:** Twitter works locally too. I follow my local petshop (@haslemerepetco) and my local cafe

(@applegarthfarm) both of which tweet their latest offers and events. I feel I know what's going on and, more importantly, spend more of my money with them because of it.

**Networking on steroids:** If you decide not to use Twitter as a direct client marketing tool (and to be honest, it's not always the most effective way of using it), then do consider using Twitter as a networking tool.

Twitter allows you to connect with local business connections as well as open up opportunities for potential joint venture relationships. I have lost count over the number of joint ventures, speaking opportunities, articles republished and journalist interest I have had because of my conversations on Twitter.

**Twitter Advanced Search:** Every tweet that is sent is published on the web, which means that every tweet has it's own specific url. If you click on the date stamp of any tweet, it will open up a new page on your browser and show the single tweet as a single web page. This means that, in theory, you can search for a specific key word phrase and if it's mentioned on that tweet, it will appear somewhere in the search results.

Now the reality is that each individual tweet does not rank very highly; each one probably not found much before search result 10,000. This is mainly because each tweet is not a well optimised page, but also because Google stopped working so closely with Twitter in 2010 because of its launch of

Google+ (ah... the politics of trying to be King of the Internet.)

But this is where Twitter Advanced Search comes in. It's a bit tricky to find, as Twitter seems to have it hidden away so the best way is to Google the phrase "Twitter Advanced Search" and you should find a link to it.

Let me give you an example of how you may want to use it. A nutritional therapist who specialises in helping people eat more healthily so they can lose weight and feel slimmer, wants to put together a group coaching programme to help ladies get into shape before their summer holidays. But before the programme gets put together and launched, the nutritional therapist needs to do a bit of market research to make sure the right content is included and there are potential clients who would buy this programme.

To find out what her target clients may be tweeting about she could go to Twitter Advanced Search and type in a key word or key phrase relating to what you want to find more about.

For this particular nutritional therapist, she could try a range of phrases such as "fat day" or "lose weight + holiday." It works just like you would use Google advanced search techniques where the plus sign will bring up tweets with both "lose weight" and "holiday" in the same tweet.

If she wanted to focus in on twitter users close to home, she could add her local city or town and choose how far a radius she would like.

You can also use negative key word phrases too by adding a minus sign before any key words so that it eliminates irrelevant tweets. This is particularly useful if you find that your tweet search just comes up with a whole load of articles tweeted from your competitors. Add the phrase "-http://*" and this will take out all tweets with any links in them and leave you with just conversational tweets to look at.

So, don't just rely on Google for the latest search results. Check out what people are tweeting about, too.

### Top tips to getting started in Twitter

**Choose a Twitter name:** Choose your own name or your business brand name, but make sure it's short and snappy enough for including on your business card or leaflets.

If your name has gone already, go for a shortened version rather than one with added numbers, for example karenskidmore78207. This just looks spammy. Plus the shorter your Twitter name is, the easier it is for your tweets to be re-tweeted (your tweet being forwarded on by one of your followers so it appears on their Twitter feed).

With only 140 characters per tweet, you can't afford to be long winded and an extra long Twitter name may end up having your tweets being shortened unnecessarily because of the 30 odd characters needed to include your @ name.

Many people do now retweet using the standard Twitter retweet which doesn't include the @ name within the 140 characters, but it's still best practice to create a short, but sweet Twitter name.

**Photo of you:** Avoid using your company logo as your avatar (the image used with each one of your tweets) and get a professional head shot done, preferably of you smiling and looking at the camera. Unless you are tweeting from a group account, you are "you" on Twitter and not a company brand, so be you in your avatar.

On some occasions, you may want to have a wacky looking avatar, for example just your eye or a profile of your nose. I know, it may sound strange but lots of people do this. As long as you are on brand with your photo (this may not work if you are an executive coach who specialises in working with CEOs of large companies, for example) then this can be a great way of having your tweets standing out from all the other lovely, smiling head and shoulder shots. If you do wacky, then just make sure it doesn't confuse your followers, or even offend them.

**Write your bio:** You have 160 characters to explain who you are. This appears on your Twitter home page, as well as any profile links when someone clicks on one of your tweets. Yes, do think about your key words that people use to find you on search engines, but write for the human beings and not the likes of Google.

Filling this space with a whole load of key word phrases just looks ugly and it does nothing to engage other human beings and encourage people to follow you.

I have seen profiles include text such as "executive coach, CEO, blue chip, Managing Directors, career coach, time management coach." They are obviously doing this style of profile for the sole purpose of getting found by people using these phrases when searching for people on Twitter. However, most people find people to follow by following tweets and recommendations rather than key word searching. If they were to check out this person's profile with all these key words slammed in their 160 characters, it doesn't exactly give any compelling reasons why they may be an interesting person to follow.

As mentioned before, you do have the opportunity to add a hyperlinked website link here, too, but avoid url shorteners here to reduce long website addresses as it will look like you are phishing or giving out dodgy links. Having two web links may confuse your Twitter followers so think before you add one.

**Decide on a tweet plan:** Plan out what sort of information you want to be tweeting about over the coming weeks. It could be a number of top tips, it could be articles listed on your website or blog, it could be links to recommended resources and websites that would be useful to your customers, it could be a combination of all these things, plus more. Brain storm and write down stuff that would be useful and of value to the people you want to reach out to.

A great way of helping you make sure you write in 140 characters is to use a spreadsheet; set up your column width to the length of 140 characters – type out 140 characters first to set this – and then you've got a benchmark to work to. It's not perfect, but it's a lot easier than writing in a Word document, I've found, plus it makes it easier to upload and schedule multiple tweets if this is something you want to do.  I'm covering content management next in this chapter, so I will be able to share plenty more on this topic, including scheduling tweets and automating your account, in a short while.

**Follow some interesting people:** The easiest way to understand how Twitter works is to start following others and see what they do. Read their tweets. Watch how they communicate with other Twitter users. See how they engage, re-tweet and reply to others.

Unlike Facebook and LinkedIn, Twitter is not a reciprocal network; you don't have to follow each other to receive each other's tweets. This is another reason why I love using Twitter so much. It means you can follow interesting people without them having to follow you back. This is a good thing; don't be so arrogant as to think that every one you follow should follow you back.

I often hear people saw that they would unfollow someone automatically if they get unfollowed by them. Why? If you don't want to read their tweets, why did you follow them in the first place? Follow people who interest you and don't worry if they follow you back or not. In my opinion, the two lists of who you follow and who follows you shouldn't have to match. Only people, who chase numbers, rather than results, worry about this.

**Tweet before you tell people:** A big mistake new tweeters make is to start telling their clients and network that they are on Twitter before they have created any tweets. Get fifteen to twenty tweets published to give people an idea on why you are on Twitter, what you tweet about and why you would be interesting enough to follow.

Once you've gone through these set up stages, have a play for a few weeks, get your head around the language used and join in with the party. Remember no one is going to come up and talk to you if you've got your arms folded, with your back to the room. The easiest way to get involved with the Twitter conversation is to start it yourself.

If you still want more tips on how to use Twitter then head on over to my Twitter Checklist for Small Businesses. You will find stacks more information, including lots of jargon busting advice. Go to www.CanDoCanBe.com/twitterchecklist to get your free copy.


## Facebook

At the time of writing, Facebook has enough registered members to make it big enough to be considered the third largest populated country in the world. What started out as a place for American college kids to arrange parties and decide which profile photo was more attractive than the other has now grown to be the largest and most dominant social network of our time.

Facebook is like a coffee morning or a visit to the local bar after work. It's full of chitchat, personal stories and observations on life. It's the place to share photos and videos, both personal and funnies from YouTube.

It's no longer just for college students. The business world started adopting Facebook as a way of connecting and communicating with contacts from about 2007 and we haven't looked back since. The demographics of the average registered user have shifted up several generations and, in fact, many teenagers today will avoid Facebook because their parents are using it; it's just not cool any more once the parents are there.

There are two main ways businesses can use Facebook: either through a personal profile or via a Facebook Page. When people connect with you via your personal profile they become your "Friend." If they come to your Facebook Page and click the "Like" button, they become a "Fan" (the Facebook Page used to be called a Fan Page, hence why the term Fans still sticks around and I don't know many people who like to use the term "Likers.")

Whichever path you take, depends on how your brand is represented and I go into more detail of this in just a moment. However, Facebook does encourage businesses to be businesses via their Facebook Pages.


**Why is Facebook such a powerful communication tool?**

**Shareability on steroids:** It seems that Facebook has taken over the internet via its Like button in recent years (and it's why Google is hitting back with its

Google+ button in an attempt to ensure its brand dominance on all things web based.)

Once you are registered on Facebook, you are able to "Like" articles and web pages on websites and blogs outside of the Facebook network and have this automatically fed into your Facebook updates. This may sound a little "Big Brother" (George Orwell … not the TV series) and there are many of you who – quite rightly – are concerned with how much information businesses such as Facebook know about your shopping habits. This type of information can be – and is - sold to advertisers and it's why you end up having very targeted Facebook adverts appearing when you are logged in to Facebook (more of how you can use this to your advantage later.)

Personal privacy issues aside for the moment, it is personal recommendations and reviews from our friends (both virtual and real-life) that are driving our personal shopping habits. It started with the likes of TripAdvisor.com and Amazon.com product reviews – all of you must have used both these sites at some point to check out specific hotels or best value digital cameras, for example - and our word-of-mouth recommendations which you all have been doing well before Facebook was created, are now being translated into clicking the Facebook "Like" buttons.

What does this shareability mean to you and your business? When someone clicks the Facebook Like button that you have put on your web page or blog article, this will show up in their newsfeed as an update for all their friends to see. Some of their friends may click the link and end up on your web page or article, which means you may have attracted a new, potentially interested client that you had no way of attracting previously.

If any of their Facebook friends visit this page in the future and are logged in to their Facebook account, this person's Facebook profile photo will be there as a "Jane Smith and three other of your friends have liked this page" link. This evidence that someone else that they know has already, in a sense, approved this page by clicking the Like button, will give them an element of confidence that this page or article is OK. This is what is called "social proof" and it's a very important element of promoting your business on the web today.

**Photo and video sharing at its best:** There are lots of photo sharing sites, such as Flickr.com, however Facebook's photo and video sharing capabilities are so easy and simple, that any of you – no matter what your technical competencies – can upload, post and share your latest pics. Whether you like it or not, you are now part of a generation who shares images of your dogs, children, funny dances, freak weather ... the list just goes on.

The cuter, freekier or funnier a photo is, the more likely it is to be shared amongst your Facebook friends.  This is why we have seen some amazing viral videos run through YouTube and fuelled by Facebook users. Just Google "Fenton the dog" – if you haven't done so already – and be amazed by the millions of views of each version of this video of a dog chasing deer across Richmond Park.

**Groups:** If you are looking to build an online community for your target clients, then diving in and creating a group could be worth checking out. Groups are used in many different ways for many different people, including private family groups for sharing photos with selected people through to clubs and sports teams to help organise events and fixtures.

Groups can be set to open (anyone and everyone can join), closed (your request to join the group has to be approved by an administrator) and secret (only those who have received an invitation to join can see or find the group.) Starting a group to help create a forum within Facebook for your target clients could be a great way of using this feature for your Facebook marketing. Done well, it can be a fantastic resource for your target clients and great PR for you and your business. However, be warned how difficult it can be to get discussion groups and forums going. There's nothing worse than speaking to yourself in an open forum all week so do think carefully about your strategy in setting one up.

**Searchability:** If you want to find someone or something, Facebook usually comes up trumps. A teacher at one of my children's schools researched the history of the school and its buildings for its 60th anniversary last year. Most of the interesting stories came via Facebook, including old photos and images for him to use in the book.

As a business owner, Facebook creates a great opportunity to "eavesdrop" on your customers' conversations and buying preferences, especially when it comes to placing adverts in front of the right people.

**Targeted advertising:** Much the same as Google Adwords work, Facebook has its own pay-per-click advertising option; you only pay for each click through on your advert, rather than on each time it appears on a page. You are able to hone in on specifics such as geographical location, age groups and which Pages they have liked.

As you can imagine, this presents you with a highly targeted advertising option that is worth exploring. You are also able to present adverts that attract "likes" for your Page, giving people the option to click "like" from the advert, rather than actually visiting your page.

If you are serious about building up a strong community within Facebook, this is one sure way to kick-start your Facebook Page to get it noticed. Just make sure you have it set up so new fans have a way of getting into your web marketing system, otherwise you could end up with an expensive advertising campaign that has made you popular but no one is buying from you.

### Top tips on getting started on Facebook

**Decide on whether to go personal profile or Page:** You have to have a personal profile set up on Facebook to be an administrator of a Page, so whether you want to use your personal profile or not, you have to have one. But you can make sure there are no direct links or connections between the two, which means you can be personally private on

Facebook, whilst still be able to build a business presence via your Page.

For most businesses, I would recommend setting up a Facebook Page for your online brand and use a personal profile to connect with associates, friends and family. Your Facebook profile is you by name and should have a photo of you, rather than a company logo. If you read the Facebook's terms of service closely, you will actually see that it is against their rules to have your business entity represented on a profile. So be very careful how you represent yourself on your personal profile if you use it to promote your business. You could find it gone one day if Facebook decide they don't like you using it the way that you are.

I do use both, although I only publicise my Facebook Page on my emails and website links. It's only natural that some of my potential clients search for me by name and want to be my friend, as this is the natural way to mutually connect with each other on Facebook. Facebook do offer a subscribe option now, which allows people to subscribe to your public feeds without being your friend but unless your target client is a whizz-kid on using Facebook, they probably won't know about this option. For me, it's about giving people the choice on how they want to connect.

But I have made a decision to avoid private updates on my personal profile. I still represent my business persona when I use my personal profile, so I avoid having pictures of my kids up there, references to holiday dates and other personal stuff. This does mean I have both my personal profile AND my Page to keep updated, so this may be too much for you.

If you do use your personal profile for "real" friends and family and want to keep it this way, set your profile privacy settings as private as possible, don't accept friend requests from people you don't know and focus your Facebook activities via your Facebook Page. There is no link between your Page and your personal profile, so you can keep a very private profile if you so wish.

**Note:** *If you do want to keep your profile private, make sure you are logged in as your Page admin before posting on your Page wall. If you haven't switched over (which you can do from your account links in the top right corner) you will be posting as "you" rather than your page. This is a common mistake that a lot of people make actually, especially if you are using the Facebook iPhone app as it only allows you to post as your profile, not as your Page admin. If you were wondering why your Page wall posts weren't being seen by your fans, check to make sure you are posting as your Page, not your profile.*

There's no real right or wrong in whether you use your personal profile and/or Page. A Facebook Page is far more effective as a business and marketing tool, but it is what's best for you, your clients and your business.

**Privacy Settings:** As much as you may hate Facebook's lack of opt-in openness (and believe me, I am not a big fan of this either), once you get into your personal privacy settings, you can be as private as you want.

When you create a new Facebook account, it will automatically be set to be as public and open as possible. I strongly recommend you get your head around how your privacy settings are set up as quickly as possible, particularly if you are using it for your "real" friends and family. Privacy settings do change as Facebook introduces new features so it's worth revisiting your settings from time to time.

Plus it's always worth checking your application privacy settings every few months too. Every time you use a new third party application – it could have been a game that you played on a company's Page or tried out a third party status scheduling tool – you would have allowed this application to access all areas of your Facebook account. You may be surprised to see dozens and dozens of such applications still getting access to your account, so go check and disable the ones that you no longer use to keep your account safe and secure.

You may also wish to opt-out of all GPS settings, which allow you to have your status updates tagged by the location you were at the time. You may not want to allow friends to tag you in photos, either – although this is a great feature if you are an avid networker and conference goer as these type of photos are a great way of connecting with your Facebook friends when you are back online.

If you are happy to be as public as possible, then that's fine. But don't assume that it's only your Facebook friends that will see what you share on

Facebook. If your settings are not how you want them, your status updates, photos and videos may be available to all and sundry once shared and tagged.

It's a common mistake I see time and time again with my friends' children's accounts. They let their child set up their own profile – or the child decides to just go ahead and set one up without their parents knowing - and it can be viewed by the world, including what school they go to and their latest wall posts organising a party that weekend. Your online privacy is your responsibility, so never assume your stuff is ever private.

**Share stuff to be shared:** As it has already been pointed out, photos and videos make Facebook tick. Be aware of this when deciding on what content to share on your Facebook Page. The right image attached to your latest blog article can make all the difference to whether anyone sees it and clicks to read it.

**Note:** *Every time you add a website link to be shared, Facebook will automatically bring in a library of images that it finds on that page. If you don't like the photo that Facebook automatically puts up for you next to the link, you can go through the library of images and chose the one that you want.*

Automatically scheduling your tweets to appear as a status update is anther bugbear of mine; although, thank goodness, this trend seems to be disappearing. Just because it's easy to do, doesn't mean you should do it. It's spammy, creates way too

218

many updates and often the Twitter jargon is totally inappropriate to the Facebook audience. If people don't unfriend you, they will most certainly hide you from their newsfeed, which defeats the object of building an online presence on Facebook.

**Note:** *If you are getting fed up with one of your friend's updates but you don't want to unfriend them, you have the option of hiding their updates from your newsfeed. This also applies to specific applications such as Farmville and Mafia Wars. If you really don't want to see what farm animals certain Facebook friends are buying and selling, then hover over the right hand corner of the update until a little settings icon appears. Click and choose the option "hide application" to make them all disappear. (I hear a sigh of relief from some of you reading this … it's great isn't it.)*

**Shared stuff is what makes Facebook work:** If your updates and content are not shared and liked, it is highly unlikely it will appear in your fans' newsfeed. The number of likes and shares is what the Facebook algorithms use to push certain updates to the top of people's newsfeeds.

Because the Facebook newsfeed for each person is defaulted to most popular updates, what most people get to see is the stuff that is shared and liked the most. Post dull stuff and updates that people are not interested in, and your communication with your Facebook audience is going to fall flat.

**Note:** *You can change this default setting of having Facebook show you the most popular instead of most recent updates. There is a settings option at the* *top right hand corner of your newsfeed. Click the icon and change over to "most recent." Facebook will keep changing it back to "most popular" for you ... as helpful as it is to make sure you see what Facebook wants you to see.*

### YouTube

So to the shiniest social media tool of them all; video. If there were one area of social media that results in more shiny toys being bought back to the nest by social media magpies, it would be the creation of videos and YouTube.

There is no doubt that video has become one of the biggest growth areas on the internet today. It's not uncommon for YouTube video links to come up on the first page of your Google searches, alongside all the relevant website links.

As more people seem to find it easier and quicker to watch a short two or three minute video having something explained to them, rather than read a one thousand word article on their screen, it is no surprise really that YouTube is now the second largest search engine after Google; which I am sure Google had planned all along being that they own them.

In 2011, fifteen hours of videos were being uploaded on to YouTube every minute, ready to be watched by hundreds of thousands of people watching millions of videos every day.

But ... there are two huge negatives when using video in your marketing. Firstly the technology around creating the videos; yes, it has never been cheaper or easier to create, edit and publish a two or three minute video. But it's easy to get sucked in and caught up with all the shiny shiny video tools and gadgets.

What starts off as a simple exercise of you talking into a web cam on your PC becomes a mammoth week long task, getting frustrated with editing software, incompatible video files and faffing about with captions & intro music. Instead of keeping to your original brief of point-and-shoot and upload, it turns you into a child hitting the sweetie shop who has just had their first taste of sugar. It's really, really easy to get carried away with what's on offer and be buying up all sort of kit and software only to complicate the whole process.

The second huge negative to using video in your marketing is that some of you should never, ever be in front of the camera. It's true, I'm afraid. Now, I am not saying you have a face made for radio but even the most normal, social people become like a rabbit frozen in headlamps when sat in front of a camera.

Come on, you must have seen some pretty darn awful "talking head" videos, haven't you? The ones who have decided to film themselves outside in the garden so all you can hear is the wind blowing through the microphone. The ones who are reading a script that they stuck just above the camera so that you can see their eyes flitting backwards and forwards whilst they grimace at the screen.

What about the ones who have the light switches just above their right ear because they haven't thought about their backdrop or the ones who look pale and sick because the lighting is all so wrong?

Video is great when it's done with proper planning and practice; but looks absolutely bloody awful when done wrong. It can kill your professionalism and reputation within three seconds of someone clicking the play button.

If you hate being in front of the camera or the thought of getting your head around cameras and video files is too much, then don't get carried away with the "must-do" YouTube attitude. Start small and practice, practice, practice, or hire an expert to help you out, especially if you are intending to create an introduction video on your home page or sales pages.

I don't want to put you off video marketing as it really is one of the most effective web tools in today's new shiny world, but I certainly don't want to see you destroy your reputation before you've even begun.

If you are a natural film star and feel comfortable in front of the camera, go for it and do it yourself. But this is one area of web marketing that is worth investing in and getting the pros to help you out. It won't be as expensive as you may think it is.

You won't need to spend thousands on an expensive film crew for a day's filming; hiring a video producer, especially one who is experienced in YouTube, is the path I would recommend most of you take to help get you started.

## Why is YouTube such a powerful communication tool?

**Get found within YouTube AND within Google searches.** If you are a nutritionist who has decided to focus on vegetarians and your target client is looking for tips on how to introduce more iron into their diet, then a short video showing them the vegetables that have a rich source of iron would have every chance of coming up on their Google search (if you have used the right key words in your tags –more info on this in a short while.)

YouTube videos are not just for YouTube, they will appear in every day Google searches, just as a blog article would.

**The "see-it-now" TV generation.** Remember the days when you only had four channels to choose from? If you were out when your favourite programme was on and you were lucky enough to have a Betamax video recorder, then you could have watched it at a later date. Ah, the good old days.

Although the majority of people who watch TV still watch it live, the trend is starting to grow for more and more people to watch programmes at a time that suits them. The few times I find myself slumping down in front of the TV I get frustrated that there is never anything I want to watch, so I am delighted with systems such as Sky+ that mean I can watch what I want, when I want.

Many TV stations are waking up to the fact that more of us want to watch whilst on the go and at times that suit us, not the programming schedules.

Websites such as BBC iPlayer and Channel 4's 4oD are hosting huge numbers of visitors daily; for example, Top Gear's Indian Special that was broadcasted in December 2011, attracted 1.7 million views in iPlayer in just two weeks.

This "see-it-now" TV generation has only fuelled our love for YouTube videos.

**A picture is worth a thousand words.** OK, this phrase is designed for images rather than videos but the same principles apply, especially if you are using video to demonstrate rather than just tell. Going back to the nutritionist, once you are confident with video, most people find it far quicker to show and talk about the vegetables that high in iron than sit down and articulate their points in an article, which may take the best part of an hour.

**One to one connection.** Reading your articles and messages is one thing, but being able to see you and hear you takes the level of engagement up several gears. People watching your videos will make snap judgments. They may take an instant dislike to you and you have got to be prepared for that. But if you are getting your messages in front of the right targeted people, seeing and hearing can quickly convert someone to trusting you very quickly.

**Multi-site sharing platform.** YouTube is a well visited social network in its own right, but because it is one of the easiest platforms to host your videos on, it allows you to share on to other social networks, such as Facebook, LinkedIn and Twitter, incredibly simply. Each video will have a short url that allows you to share via your tweets and updates, or you can use the sharing buttons that YouTube make available under each video.

The video url can also be used to share your videos on your website and blog. If you are using WordPress, there are plenty of plugins that allow you to copy and paste code to publish it on your web page very easily. The benefit of using YouTube to host your video – i.e. the person who sees it on your website or blog actually views the video through a window on your web page and views it directly on YouTube - is that it won't slow your own website down. Videos hosted on your site can be the quickest way to make your website pages slow to load; a definite no-no especially when more people are viewing via smart phones and tablets wirelessly.

**Note:** *YouTube videos don't always have to be set as public videos and be found on the massive YouTube directory. You have the option of making a video totally private or even viewable only by people who have the link. What this means is you can use YouTube to host your free offer, which may be in the form of a video course, but only those who subscribe via your opt-in page on your website and then sent the links will be able to view the videos.*

### Top tips on getting started on YouTube

**Create your own channel.** When you set up an account on YouTube, you are given your own channel that you can brand and format to suit your needs. YouTube have different options for you to set your channel "home page" up, as well being able to choose colours and add your company logo.

**Start subscribing to other people's channels.** You can get great ideas on what sort of videos to create once you begin to realise what is possible. Search for your competitors or other businesses in similar industries and see what they are publishing.

**Tag your videos.** When you write and publish articles, Google is able to "read" the text and find relevant key word matches to enable your article to appear in searches. It's not possible to do this with a video file – yet – so to make sure your videos can get found by the likes of Google and YouTube, you need to add text for them to index.

The title of your video is very important, just like the title of your blog article. It's the headline to get people to watch but it's also important indexing text. But you also need to add tags – key word phrases – to your video when uploading it. So think how your target clients may want to find this video and which phrases they would be using when searching.

**Tell people what to do next.** Unless the people who watch your videos are psychic, they won't know what website or opt-in report you want them to visit or sign up for unless you tell them. Be specific and give them an easy website address for them to remember because if they've heard it, they will be typing it … not clicking it. So remember the dedicated domains I mentioned before. This is a great time to use them.

Another thing to do is to add annotations and/or title pages. It's good practice to add the website address to the video as an annotation at the point that you say it, as well as adding it at the end as a title page along with the reason for going there.

You can use video editing software to do this, but YouTube gives you the options to add annotations right there and then in your account. Once you've uploaded the video, click on the edit link and you will find an amazing collection of edit features, including adding annotations.

As you get more advanced in your knowledge of YouTube, you can start adding clickable links to your video which means that someone watching your video can click the video and be taken directly to the page you are talking about; but one step at a time. I told you that YouTube is very shiny, didn't I?

**Add your website links to your description box.** When you upload your video, you also have the option of adding a description of what the video is all about. Not only is this useful for helping people decide whether they should watch it or not, but this box also allows you to add a hyperlinked (clickable) website address.

The link needs to have the "http://" in front of the "www" to make this link is clickable and I would also recommend you add your link right at the start of the description. If you have a long description and put your link at the bottom, you run the risk of it disappearing beneath the "show more" tab.

Plus, when your video appears in a Google search, the first 100 or so characters of the description appear on the search results. So make sure these first few characters are as enticing as possible as it will help encourage more people to click through to your video, as opposed to someone else's.

**Keep your videos short and sweet.** Two or three minutes are plenty long enough if you want to grab someone's attention and share something of value. People have short attention spans online, in particular when using social networks, so unless you are offering some fantastic "must watch" stuff, then anything over three minutes is going to bore people and they won't watch to the end.

**Professional but amateur.** Be business professional when in front of the camera, but don't think you have to be video professional. Most of your target clients are not going to expect – nor want – Spielberg quality. If you use a good quality camera (a Flip or your iPhone 3 and above camera are plenty good enough) good lighting (natural daylight is great but direct sunshine not) and a good quality microphone (a light background hissing can ruin a video … and avoid the outside if it is windy, too) then you should be all set.

**It's not all about talking heads.** The place most people start with creating videos is to record themselves talking at the camera. But there are so many other options you can do.

Camtasia, which is the popular video creating and editing tool that a lot of people end of getting, is expensive if you just want to give a couple of videos a go. Start with Jing, which is a stripped down version of Camtasia (owned by the same people) and gives you the ability to record videos of up to five minutes. Jing is perfect for screen sharing and demonstrating a "how to" video as you talk someone through what you are showing them on your PC screen. For example, you could give people a tour of a particular website; even your own if that's something that is of value to a new visitor.

If you prefer to stay away from the camera but feel happy to talk, why not use slides with images and/or bullet points and record a voice-over. This is can be done with Jing, too.

There are also great video creation sites, such as Animoto.com, that give you the opportunity to upload images, text, audio and even music (or use one of the files from Animoto's extensive library) to create a montage based video that you don't even have to appear live in.

There are even cartoon and animation websites popping up giving non-technical people like you affordable ways of creating videos with a difference.

---

**MAGPIE ALERT**

*Be careful not to spend all your time on creating and forgetting what your business objectives are. If you want to "play" with these shiny toys, then leave it for your downtime and weekends.*

**Practice, practice, practice.** People often ask me how I can talk to a camera and come across so natural. It wasn't like that to start with, I can assure you. In fact, you may still be able to find some dodgy looking clips from the early days if you go through my YouTube playlists. Feeling relaxed in front of a camera takes practice and if you need to write out a script and rehearse it for an hour or two to start with, then do it.

That's exactly how I started and yes, it took a long while for a two minute video to get filmed. But after lots of practice, I can scribble down some notes, run through it once and then hit record for a one take finish. So you will get better over time.

If you really do struggle, then take up my earlier suggestion and contact an expert. A good video person will relax you, feed you questions if that makes it easier for you talk and edit out all the bits that you stumble with or go wrong.

### Niche forums and networks

We've just gone through the four biggest and most talked about social media networks, but you may find that your clients hate Twitter but spend two or three hours a week logged on to an industry specific discussion forum. They may turn their nose up to Facebook but are very active in a private online club.

For example, the French don't seem to use sites such as LinkedIn. They hang out in Viadeo. German speaking countries focus their online networking on Xing. If you are looking to engage and reach out to the "mummy network," they are hanging out in forums such as NetMums.com.

Remember to look beyond the Big Four and ask your clients where else they choose to spend their internet time. You may be amazed how many specific niche discussion groups, other online networking sites and online clubs there are for your target clients.

## How to sell on social media

Keeping the balance between value and selling is incredibly important when it comes to sharing content across your social media networks. During the blogging chapter, I explained the difference in writing for your website to writing for your blog. This applies here, too. Your style of writing and what you share needs to reflect the platforms you are on.

If you want it in percentage terms, I recommend:

70% value (your blog articles, tips, how-to videos, retweets and shares of others' blog articles)

20% personal (what you had for lunch, comments on the weather, opinions on a TV show)

10% selling (links to promotions, events, new products)

Once you get in the flow, you won't need to be so conscious about this split. You'll begin to work out just what's appropriate to build those relationships with your online network. Over promote and you will see people unfollowing, unfriending or hiding you in their newsfeeds. Not promote enough and

you will get lots of lovely things said about you ...
but not enough clients coming through.

You'll learn what the right balance is for your
clients. But how do you make sure you are getting
results from your social media activity?

## How do you actually sell on social media?

Including the words "Selling" and "Twitter" in the
same sentence can send some social
media enthusiasts into an anaphylactic shock. It's
the same with Facebook. Some Facebook users are
incredibly protective over their social space and
will rant and rage at the mere thought of a business
talking business.

Social media is social in its very nature and if you
were to start touting your wares like a double
glazing salesman, then no one would want to be
social with you.

LinkedIn is the exception; being a business network,
it is expected that you share business stuff. The
reverse is true if you try to be too social and only
share videos of talking cats via your LinkedIn
updates. But hard selling on sites such as Twitter
and Facebook is similar to the person you meet at a
networking event who seems more intent on
thrusting over his business card to everyone in the
room and talking "at" you, than having a
conversation "with" you.

But if you can't sell on Twitter and Facebook, why
use them as a business tools?

First of all, let's dispel the myth that all marketing is selling. Selling happens when a potential client expresses an interest in what you do and wants to make a decision on how much money to spend with you. They may ask you about the price of an event, they may call you up asking about timeframes and delivery options. They want to buy and you are there to sell to them. But this process doesn't happen at the beginning.

Very rarely does your potential new client phone you up on that very first contact – whether it's a tweet, email or website link from a Google search - and give you a brief on what they need and ask when you will start working on their project.

For most of you, they may cruise through your website. They may search for you by name to check out any reviews online. They may sign up for your free offer, follow you on Twitter and read your emails for a few months.

This whole process of engagement, building trust and rapport happens over time – sometimes a few weeks, sometimes a few years. And it's this communication that is marketing, as the selling only happens when they are ready to buy.

So, the question of how do you sell on social media really should be re-phrased to become "how do you engage on social media?" And isn't it much easier to think about how to engage, rather than to sell?

Ask me to directly sell on Twitter and I could give you examples of tweets that involve lots of "Special discount on membership if you buy today" or

"Three for the price of two if you click here right now." By all means, tweet these from time to time.

There's no such thing as the Twitter police and you are not going to get thrown in Twitter jail for tweeting this kind of stuff … contrary to some social media evangelists' belief.

But, tweet like this all day and Twitter is going to be a very lonely place for you. It is the same in Facebook, too. You are going to get unfriended and unliked very quickly.

Ask me to engage on Twitter and I can give you examples of tweets that involve "Can't believe they killed off Harry on Silent Witness" (that conversation lasted all day – if you are a fan of Silent Witness, do you remember that episode? Cracker, wasn't it?) or "KitKat or Hobnob? What should I have with my cup of tea?" (biscuit tweets are great fun and involve lots of banter.)

But Harry from Silent Witness and KitKats don't sell my business. I know that. But the relationships you build up with people who follow you and how you engage with each other, do.

And that's how you sell on social media. The 20% of personal stuff is really important small talk that you all do in "real-life" to start relationships with people – both business and personal – and you need to make sure you are doing it on social media, too.

There are lots of people who scoff about the banality of Twitter, in particular … but it works.

## How public do you need to be about your private stuff?

OK, so if small talk works, how personal do you get with your online network?

It seems that when it's just us and our smart phones, it's easy to forget that the messages we send out on Twitter or Facebook can reach anyone, anywhere in the world. A drunken Friday night tweet seems funny at the time ... but what if one of your clients sees it whilst sitting on their sofa at home?

Ignoring emails from a client who is complaining about one of your products, whilst glibly updating your Facebook status with a "Don't you just hate it when someone moans all the time and is not happy with what they get" is going to have you skating on very thin ice.

You've all seen the kind of headlines that appear in the tabloids from drunken celeb tweets or sports personalities speaking out of turn about a private matter on a very public platform. A tweet can move faster across the internet than a rocket into space and once shared and retweeted, it is almost impossible to retract.

Just think back to the ridiculous gagging orders over stuff shared on Twitter that we've had here in the UK over the past couple of years.

But does this mean you should be afraid of sharing too much private stuff on your public profiles? As just explained, if you just stick to business all the time and just try to sell, the "social" side of social media ignores you. So, how public do you need to be about your private stuff to make social media work for your business?

There are three categories that I think most of your thoughts, feelings and ideas fit into:

**1. Public:** this is all the information that is about your business, your events and your products. This includes launches of new programmes or workshops, appointments of new staff, winning new projects or new articles on your blog. It's all the stuff you really want potential clients reading about you and your business.

It tends to be the positive news you want to share, although every cloud usually has a silver lining so don't be afraid of sharing bad news if you can find a way to add value from it. Avoid the doom and gloom, but sometimes an honest bit of commentary makes you a "real" business.

**2. Public Private:** the information you want to share with the world about you as a person. This includes your personal thoughts about the latest industry developments, conferences or events you go to and what you had for lunch.

Yes, that's right – what you had for lunch. As already explained, small talk is necessary to start relationships, both personal and business. It's how we are as human beings. If you think about what you talk about when having "small talk" with someone you've just met, the topics usually focus on the weather (well, for Brits), where you're off on your hols this summer and what drink or food you are currently consuming.

So when people who just don't get Twitter and question whether anyone could possibly be interested in whether you had a bacon sandwich or a bowl of soup today, it's because "small talk" is important.

Do it all day and every day, and it is very boring. But make your public profiles a little private – share a "secret" or a personal fact about yourself – and you are able to show you are a human being and a very nice person to be doing business with.


**3. Private:** information that your clients really don't need to know about you. This includes your kids' names, your car registration number plate, your home number and the name of your bank. Some of you, I know, do share stuff like your kids' names. And that's OK as long as you consider this to be Public Private stuff and you don't mind the whole world knowing this.

Announcing when you plan to go away on holiday is a common crime, especially if you work from home. Why not just tell the local thief network when your house if going to be vacant?

You want to avoid sharing anything that may cause clients to leave you in droves. Remember the comment Gerald Ratner made about his jewellery in 1991? It caused the company to go from a £112 million profit to a £122 million loss a year later. And that was all before the shareability of social media.

I have a little rule when it comes to sharing stuff: if it ends up on the front page of the Sun or the Times, I wouldn't be worried if my mum were to see it.

You can be as public or as private as you want to be on social media – the choice is yours. But just be prepared if what you share does get found.

If you want it kept private, then avoid those drunken Friday tweets and early morning Facebook rants.

## Creating content to share on social media

So you've got your blog articles, you've got your own personal updates to share and you've got news and commentary about your own business and the industry that you are in. But if you try to come up with all your own material, all of the time, it can get very wearing.

This is where you can dive into other people's content and share without having to create any of it. Sharing other people's updates and articles is what social media thrives on. It spreads the word about other people, which means other people will share your updates and content in return and spread the word about you.

Sharing other people's content also raises your expert status. It may not be your original content (and you certainly shouldn't be passing it off as your own) but people will perceive you to be the font of all knowledge so will use you as their "Google." It means they will be more likely to sign up for your free offers and enjoy receiving your emails.

Here are some ideas.

**YouTube videos:** What interests your target clients? Is it easy recipes for working mums? Is it golf techniques and putting skills? Is it the latest key note speech from leaders in your industry? I can guarantee that whatever it is, you will find dozens and dozens of videos on YouTube about whatever topic you search for. And Facebook users, in particular, loooooove their videos.

**Latest news:** Surf the national and international news sites – BBC, Daily Mail or Guardian. What headlines are worth sharing and commenting on? Copy the link to that specific article or use the social share buttons on the sites.

**Other people's blog articles:** If you aren't subscribing to the top blogs in your profession, then get to it. Set up a free account with Google and use their Google Reader account to subscribe to the blogs that you find. Once a week (or once a day – depending on your routine) scan through the articles and share the good ones with your network.

**Other Facebook Page's Updates:** When you are logged in as your Page admin, you can Like other Pages as your Page. Updates from these Pages will appear in your Page's Newsfeed, when you log in as your Page. This is a really great way of building collaborative relationships on Facebook and getting your Page known to their fans.

Add your own comments on original update so it appears on the other Page's wall for their fans to see, share the update on your own page and even use the magic tag key to link the other person's Page your status update. To use this tag key, simply click the @ symbol and start typing the Page name immediately after. If you have Liked their page, a list of Pages should appear as you type and you can select the Page you want tagged to the update.

Do use this tag feature selectively. When you tag, Facebook automatically adds your status update to their wall so if you go overboard, it may come across as spamming and this won't do your relationship with the other Page's administrator any good.

## Automating – the good, bad & ugly

If you are busy with client projects, why not just get your social media accounts automated? What could be easier than setting and forgetting your accounts so you are keeping your potentially interested clients updated, whilst you are busy at work?

Great concept and yes, there is a certain amount of automation you can set up. But set and forget and never bother to check, can work against you.

Here's a quick example. Not so long ago I tweeted about my new Dog Rocks. For those of you with dogs and get fed up with those little burnt patches of grass from their pee spots, there are some rocks you can put in their water to neutralize their pee. I know, sounds ridiculous, but they really do work. I tweeted about my Dog Rocks and noticed the next day that Dog Rocks were on Twitter and had followed me.

I hate it when I get auto-followed by porn stars and iPad resellers, but somehow getting auto-followed by Dog Rocks made me smile. So I followed them back and sent them a public message but I got nothing back. I got ignored. The account had been set up as a robotic auto-follow and tweets were scheduled to go out ... but no human interaction was happening to respond to any replies they were getting. I still buy my Dog Rocks but if another product came around that was cheaper or better, I wouldn't think twice about changing, as I feel no loyalty to the brand.

If they had engaged with me, I may have felt differently. Hopefully they have changed now and put a human being on their Twitter account.

Set-and-forget marketing is great. In fact, some set-and-forget marketing is critical to profitability ... and sanity. Just flip back to the section on autoresponders and you will remember how critical I feel they are to a small business like yours. But be careful how much you automate in networks such as LinkedIn, Twitter and Facebook.

## What automation is good?

There is a certain amount of automation that is needed, especially when you are busy. Here are some ideas on what you can do ... in moderation.

**Scheduled updates from social media dashboards:** There are several social media dashboards for you to choose from that work as third party tools to help you manage your social networking accounts. Hootsuite, Tweetdeck and SocialOmph are the three main players at the time of writing but there are others to check out depending on your requirements and usability.

These social media dashboards make managing your social networking accounts easier by allowing you to manage all your accounts from under one roof. Many people find the Twitter interface rather two dimensional, even with its recent facelifts. And if you are managing an active LinkedIn profile and several Facebook Pages, then it makes sense to work in one place to improve your time management.

One of the big advantages of using one of these social media dashboards is the ability to schedule updates – tweets, wall posts on your Facebook Page, LinkedIn updates – for specific times and days in the future. Some offer free scheduling options and some are chargeable, depending on how many accounts you run and whether you want to upload large number of tweets and updates quickly, rather than individually add and schedule. So it's up to you whether you want to pay.

As with Goldilocks and her morning porridge, too much sugar can be too sweet and too much salt makes it sour; and you may lose your followers quicker than you attract them. "Just right" is to keep yourself noticed and create online conversations (replies, comments and likes) whilst you are busy with your day job.

How many updates you can automate during the day will depend on the number of followers you have, the number of blog posts you publish and the number of times a day you personally jump in and interact. Test for yourself.

And if you have an international audience, it may make sense to schedule updates whilst you sleep, as your overseas followers may not be awake when you are, thus not see you in their newsfeeds.

**Notification of new blog articles:** As your blog is run on something called RSS (really simple syndication) this can be used to alert any of your social networks and get a link to your blog article published on any of your profiles or pages. There are a number of ways of doing this – Hootsuite, Tweetdeck, Twitterfeed or NetworkedBlogs. It's classic set-and-forget marketing activity.

However, just because you can, doesn't always mean you should.

For example, I've stopped automatically feeding my blog articles into my Facebook Page and now add them as a manual wall post. This allows me to add a personal comment or ask a question alongside the link. The more personal you can be within sites such as Facebook, the better results you get. Plus, Facebook keep changing the way its newsfeed algorithms work and it is recommended that manual wall postings get placed higher than wall postings through third party applications. This is a much debated topic but it is something that needs to be considered in your decision to automate or not.

However, I know that not everyone has the time or motivation to manually post. And if you don't have the time, nor have the resources to have this delegated to someone else, then better to set-and-forget, and then forget to post anything at all.

**Ad hoc scheduling:** As you start to read blogs and surf around to find good content to share on your social networks, you may find that there will be days that you share like crazy and other days that you just don't. It would be lovely to have an hour a day to focus on what's going on with the latest news and some of you may find that this is an hour well worth spending each and every day.

However, for many of you this simply will be a luxury and will be hard to keep up. What tends to happen is that you have an hour one Monday, for example, that you find loads of great stuff, you share away and send out a dozens of so tweets or updates … and then nothing for the rest of the week. It is far better to drip feed slowly and steadily over a period of days and weeks if you can.

Now you could be super efficient and add each article link that you want to share into your schedule on your social media dashboard account. But this can take a while. This is where a lovely tool called Buffer.com comes in. Buffer allows you to share the page, but on a drip-fed basis. If you have an hour or so finding great articles, add them to your Buffer account via a "share this" button you can add to your web browser and Buffer will feed out your updates to the schedule you've set

244

i.e. every four hours and only between 7am and 9pm your time. Neat, hey?

**Tweet Old Post:** I wanted to avoid writing about specific tools during this social media chapter because of the fear that as soon as this book is printed, they may have gone. And there is nothing more frustrating than reading a book and finding out something that has been recommended is no longer in use. But there is one more tool I really want to share with you here and I hope it's around for a very long time.

Tweet Old Post is a WordPress plugin – so it can only be used on WordPress.org websites, I'm afraid – and syncs with your Twitter account to tweet old blog posts. It's great to get your latest new article sent out, but what about all the other great stuff you've written over the last few months and years? This is where this plugin is fantastic and it's simply amazing at rejuvenating old blog posts and driving more interested people back to your blog.

### Where next?

OK, let me draw an end to this chapter on social media. I could keep writing and writing and writing, but the purpose of this book is not to show everything and anything there is to know and do on social media. There are plenty more advanced strategies and techniques I could share with you … but you don't want to become a social media magpie, do you?

The purpose of this book is to show you the steps and stages of web marketing that you need to take, and thus enable you to see the results from social media marketing. Every journey starts with a single step and if you try to "do it like the gurus" and expect your social media campaigns to go viral when you take your first few steps, you'll be sorely disappointed.

Get the basics right, do the hard graft and homework on which social networks you want to start with and you will see results.

Now before you go and put this book away and get on with your web marketing set up, I really want you to shine.

# STEP SEVEN
## BEING SHINY SHINY

Congratulations! You have read through the six steps and you are almost at the end of this book. I have hopefully inspired you and opened your eyes to what web marketing systems you can create. Being successful on social media is possible but, as you have read, you need a well thought out house and engine room working hard in the background to make sure you reap the benefits of your virtual network of connections.

Whatever profession or industry you are in, I can bet your marketplace is very, very crowded. It's not just the big players you up against, either. As more and more people make the decision to start up on their own, hundreds, if not thousands, of new start-ups join the front lines and jostle for positions to get in front of your target clients every year.

As each year passes, it gets harder to be a beacon in your crowded marketplace, which makes social media marketing even more critical to get right. The soft glowing porch light you switch on over your front door to welcome potential visitors into your website, fades away in comparison when your neighbour next door turns on their flashing neon "special offer" signs.

Garish, flashing neon signs aren't always the solution, but you can't rely on that porch light glowing softly in the distance to hope that one day, some one will pass and decide to knock on your door. You will get one or two clients from your porch light, absolutely. But do you want a business that ends up being an expensive hobby? Or do you want a business that generates income constantly and consistently throughout the year and gives you the freedom to make choices on what you do and when?

To rise above the crowds and stand out from all the rest, you have to shine as bright as a beacon to make sure your target clients are attracted to you; like moths on a dark, summers night.

But I know that there will be many of you who may be feeling ever so slightly overwhelmed at the mountainous task ahead of you. Whether you already have a blog or an email newsletter set up, you are probably not using it in the ways that I have outlined in this book.

There seems a mighty lot of work ahead … so perhaps it's just easier to shove this book on your bookshelf and go back to tweeting and facebooking the way that Rebecca and Simon were doing in the story at the start of this book. After all, it may better to have a couple of potential clients every month to feel like you still have a business, than roll up your sleeves and risk none of it working.

That's OK, because I can't hold a gun to your head to make you do any of these steps outlined in this book. I can't force you to make changes and take action to get results from your social media marketing. You may be completely content with being an expert on Twitter and an ever-increasing credit card debt.

I can't give you a magic wand, either. There is no pill you can swallow or bag of fairy dust to sprinkle over your desk to get your website, blog, email newsletters and opt-in offers all working for you.

The reality is that it is up to you. You need to put the hard graft in to get it started and get it working. It's great being your own boss and feeling the freedom of being able to do what you want, when you want. But the flip side is that it's down to you to do what you want, when you want. If you want – and maybe even need – your social media marketing to see results, you have to be the one to take ownership and get things moving.

But there is some good news.

You don't have to do this alone.

## Just because you can, doesn't mean you should

One of the big problems with using the shiny new tools that social media offer is the technical knowhow and mindset needed to get yourself up and running. It's not as if you have to be a computer programmer to set up accounts (although it probably feels like it at times) but you do need to step back and ask yourself if you the right person to be doing it.

You are good at certain things; there is no question about that. It may be that you are top coach, an incredible therapist or an amazing trainer that guarantees results. But there are a few things that I bet you know little about; for example getting your landing page working on your Facebook Page, syncing your blog with your Twitter account, adding YouTube videos to your blog.

Yes, you can learn. Yes, you probably could give it a go and get it done … all by yourself. But how many hours (and how much cursing) will it take for you to do it?

Whether you charge yourself out at £35 an hour or £2,500 a day, I can guarantee that there will be someone out there who could do it for you for less than your hourly rate. And, quite possibly, get the whole task done in a quarter of the time that it takes you to find a "how-to" video to watch and learn from YouTube.

Your role in the business is not to be the Marketing Assistant. You are the Marketing Director and take responsibility for your overall marketing strategy, but your role is to focus on what you are good at and drive your business forward, rather than tinkering around with finding the right images to go with your latest blog post. Delegate as much as you can and you'll see better results, faster.

### When is the right time to hire a virtual assistant?

First of all, let's just explain what a virtual assistant is for those of you who haven't come across this term. A virtual assistant (VA) is some one who carries out admin, technical or project based work assignments for you on a contractual basis. They work remotely – hence the term virtual – so, in most cases, you don't have to have someone physically come to your home or office to carry out the tasks you want to them to do. In many cases, you may never meet your VA; I know I will probably never meet Cathy who is my technical support and membership co-ordinator for my Web Tech Club because she is based in Texas and I live in the South East of England.

A VA does not appear on your payroll, which means that you don't have to get bogged down with complicated red tape or expensive employee benefits such as sick pay, maternity pay or redundancy. They are usually paid by the hour so you only pay them for the work that they do … and not for the two week holiday they take in the summer.

If you run out of work to pass to them, or even feel the pinch for a couple of months and have to cut back on your outgoings, then there is no notice period or redundancy benefits to be paid (although if you have signed a long term contract with your VA, you may need to give them a one month's notice depending on the terms of service you have agreed.)

A VA can offer you short term, quick fix solutions and help with your projects, for example setting up your autoresponder account and designing a newsletter template. Or a VA can work with you as a member of your team and build an on-going business relationship, for example being your personal assistant and managing your social media accounts.

It was more than five years ago that I took on my first VA and I remember the struggle and confusion I felt when I first decided to take the plunge. You see,

I bet we are alike. You run your own business. And you probably are, like all good entrepreneurs and business owners, a bit of a control freak.

When it's your business - your clients, your blood, sweat and tears - it's really hard to start handing over some of that responsibility to someone else. Someone who – let's be frank here – you are not sure you can really trust. What happens if they send out the wrong email to the wrong person? What happens if they end up offending a new client that results in them cancelling the contract you've just agreed?

What happens if they start tweeting inappropriate tweets or delete your Facebook Page by mistake?

All over-the-top, drama-queen emotions, yet perfectly reasonable thoughts from a business owner like you and me. But if you carry on running the business in the same way you are at the moment and you try to set up and manage all the web marketing systems that I have outlined in this book, you probably know that you are going to drop some balls yourself. Trying to do it all by yourself is guaranteed to result in you being the person who sends out the wrong email and messing up your Facebook account.

So when is the right time to take on some extra help and hire a VA? Here are some of the danger signs:

**You have become a slave to your inbox.** Every time you respond to an email another five magically appear, which means you never have a chance to get on with planning out your free offer. Or writing this months blog articles that you promised to do this week.

**You are missing messages on your phone.** You are out with clients and it takes you at least three days before you manage to phone someone back … and you are losing potential new projects on the way.

**You are spending hours sending out information to clients** such as training packs, terms of engagement letters, quotes and proposals. You sit by the printer waiting patiently for everything to come off before you dash to the post office to get it in the last post of the day.

**You have projects** such as "set up email newsletter" or "get Facebook Page sorted" **on your to-do-list for week after week**.

**You find yourself sat at your desk on a Saturday morning** working out the last six months of business receipts whilst your family goes out for a day trip to a local park.

**You are missing out on having that "every other Friday" that you promised yourself** to spend with friends – working for yourself meant that you were you own boss … but it feels like you are chained to your laptop and can't get away.

**You are frustrated by your website** as several of the pages are so out of date that you have stopped sending potential clients there to look at it.

And the reason why I know these danger signs is because I have had them all at some point in my own business. By the time I came round to getting someone in to help with my business, I was in such a whirlwind of thoughts and big ideas that trying to explain what I needed help with was tough. When it's all in your head and you've trained yourself to think "it's quicker if I just get on and do it" – you know you've got to slam on the breaks and take the time out to get some help. Because if you don't you will only end up suffocating your own success.

So, when is it the right time to get a VA? It's before you begin that new Facebook project. It's before you decide to launch your new free offer. And it's before you launch yourself into a frenzy of project juggling.

As you go through each of the steps outlined in this book, you can break off one small chunk at a time – such as creating your free offer, writing and scheduling your email newsletter or setting your scheduled tweets – and focus on getting help on this. If you do, you will find it far easier than trying to get help with the mountainous task of setting up your web marketing systems. Plus you will have stronger foundations to take on more clients and projects without taking more of your precious time to do it.

It can take three or four months to establish a good working relationship with a VA but once it's there, the sense of freedom is wonderful. Knowing that there is someone else to do the things you hate to do and not able to do so you can concentrate on what really matters.

If you are serious about hiring a VA – and why wouldn't you not be – but still feel stuck on how and where to start, then check out my short online course that will show you exactly what to do to find the right VA for you and your business. Go to www.candocanbe.com/howtohireava for more information.

## Using other people's beacons

Having someone helping you out with the technical set up is a great start to getting you on the road to social media success. But there are also other easier paths to follow.

You may be just you in your business. You may build a VA team and end up having more than one person helping you out and supporting your online presence. However, it's still just you who creates, delivers and supports your clients. But what if I was to suggest that you go out there and find other businesses to work with ... even direct competitors?

What? Isn't doing business with your competitors crazy?

Did you know that one of the quickest ways of attracting new clients to your business is to use other businesses' databases? And that even includes using your direct competitors.

Now I am not suggesting in the slightest that you are to break in to their offices overnight and steal their client information. But what I am suggesting is that you collaborate and look at what joint ventures you can create. Joint ventures are when two [or more] businesses join forces to create a more powerful force in the marketplace. Think of it as two heads are better than one; or more importantly, two databases are better than one.

Let me give you an example. Dan is a coach who specialises in working with other coaches who need mentoring on their coaching skills. He's been established for twenty odd years and grew a solid reputation for being one of the top go-to guys to help newly trained coaches gain further professional accreditation. The problem is that when Dan first started, attracting enough clients was easy but now the marketplace is crowded and he's just not getting the referrals like he used to. He's still just as good, but he's only got a softly glowing porch light switched on.

He's put together a great website, come up with a stonking good free offer and decided to get stuck into Facebook as this is where many of his clients seem to be networking and hanging out. He starts off well and gets his first one hundred fans fairly easily, but he hasn't managed to get above this magic one hundred mark for the past four months. Although he's got the right marketing systems set up, he's feeling deflated because he's simply not getting in front of enough people.

Rather than give up, this is when Dan decides to look around and see who else works with his target clients. There are plenty of other businesses all vying for the attention of newly qualified coaches but Dan takes the time to research and check out who would be his top five businesses to reach out to.

He reads their blogs, he signs up for their newsletters and he takes time to understand how the other businesses like to work with their clients. He decides to approach a NLP training school; he puts together an email explaining how he may be able to help them out in what they are trying to achieve. You see, it's all about the other person; what's in it for them?

He reckons that if he can support their students through their NLP training courses with his supervised coaching, more of their students would finish the course and this would improve their referral rates. He presents them with his free offer that he has on his website and explains why each of their students would benefit from receiving it.

That email leads to several phone discussions, a face-to-face meeting and the NLP training company agreeing to link with Dan's Facebook Page and an email marketing campaign promoting his free offer to their database.

OK, so this story is hypothetical. This could be too crazy for a lot of NLP training companies who just wouldn't entertain this idea and turn Dan down flat. After all, shouldn't they be offering their own mentoring and supervised coaching service? But we are in a very interesting economy at the moment. Sticking with the norm and assuming that a particular business will not want to talk to you is frankly madness.

Many businesses are experiencing huge slowdowns and one of the advantages to you is that slowdowns cause problems. If you can solve the right problems, it's good for your business; and, of course, good for the other businesses, too.

More and more businesses are looking at joint ventures and building collaborative partnerships – even with direct competitors. So doing business with your competitors really isn't such a crazy idea.

The trick is being able to create an offer that benefits both parties, plus their clients.

Social media presents you with an enormous opportunity to seek out and connect with potential partners. You really don't have to struggle on by yourself to attract the right clients to your Facebook Pages and your free offers. Joint ventures could be the quickest - and cheapest - way of moving your business forward right now.

Who could you start connecting with and talking to so you can create a win-win situation for you both?

## Is it time to ditch traditional marketing?

This book is all about web marketing and social media. You are now part of this shiny new world and there's no going back. Embrace it or find your beacon slowly fading and your target clients ignoring you.

But now that you have all these web based marketing tools, does that mean traditional marketing, such as printed brochures, face-to-face networking and advertising are things of the past? Can't you just ditch all that expensive stuff and put all your energies into these new web tools?

It's tempting isn't it?

But be tempted and you'll probably find yourself left with a very quiet business pipeline. You know by now how effective websites, blogs, email marketing and social media can be but use them in isolation, turn your back on the more traditional marketing activities and you could lose a lot of business.

Behind my very visible web presence lies speaking schedules, regular face-to-face networking, newsletters as well as postcard campaigns, magazine articles and word of mouth referrals to name but a few other offline marketing activities I embrace. I may be considered to be an expert in web marketing tools but I'm not an internet marketer. I'm a business owner who uses internet marketing strategies.

Let me give you a great example of a marketing campaign run by the number one market leader of the internet - Google. When Google released its own internet browser, Chrome, in 2009 you expected an online campaign. But did it rely only on the internet? Absolutely not.

They took out full page spreads in national papers. They were on billboards up and down the country. They had posters in and around the underground in London. They had a full scale, offline advertising campaign going and all to spread the word of an internet based product, that could only be used on the internet.

So, it's not a case of choosing between using social media and traditional methods. It's about integrating the two worlds together and making sure your offline world is backing up what you are doing online, and vice versa.

How do you do this? Here are a few simple suggestions to think about - none of which involved a national advertising campaign, you'd be relieved to know.

Have the web addresses of your online profiles on your business card, along with your phone number and business address – give people the option of how they want to get in touch with you.

Arrange to have a coffee meeting with a new contact you "meet" on LinkedIn – get to really know your online network.

Have your phone number listed on your website, blog and social networking profiles – make it easy for people to speak to you, rather than be forced to message you electronically all the time.

Pick up the phone to someone rather than send them a message online – it's amazing what these conversations can lead to.

Follow up the people you've met at a networking event and search for them on LinkedIn – get connected online with the people you meet offline.

Use postcards to promote your Facebook Page or LinkedIn group to encourage more people to visit and sign up – don't just rely on those automatic email invitations that seemed to get ignored most of the time.

These are just a few ideas to get you going and very few of them need any cash to follow them through.

Don't get caught up with the sparkles and glitz of social media and ignore your offline strategies.

The more you can integrate your social media marketing with your traditional marketing, the more effective it will be.

**Final words ...**

Thank you for reading this book and I hope you feel more confident in getting your social media marketing working. I'm sure you feel there's a lot for you to do but if there is just one thing I want you to take away from this book it is this ... you need to own your client database.

Your social media marketing will not work in the long term, or the short term to be honest, if you act like a tenant and allow Facebook, Twitter, LinkedIn and YouTube to be your landlord.

As coaches, trainers and consultants, the biggest and most valuable asset that you will ever have will be your database so make sure you put the right web marketing strategies in place to make that happen.

# About The Author

Karen Skidmore, founder of CanDoCanBe and creator of the Web Tech Marketing Club, is a marketing mentor and self-confessed web tech geek. A practical, down-to-earth business woman, Karen excels at making web tech marketing tools simple and accessible to small business owners, so that you can attract the right clients constantly and consistently throughout the year.

Having left an eleven year corporate career when her eldest daughter started school, she started up initially as a life coach in 2004. After just five months, Karen realised how tough it was to start a part-time business when you were selling yourself. Rather than give up, she re-evaluated her marketing and started to explore the world of the internet.

Starting her first email newsletter and launching her first blog in 2005, Karen's online presence has grown and grown. And it was only natural that she became an early adopter of social media tools such as Twitter, Facebook, LinkedIn and YouTube. Over the years, more and more business owners have sought out Karen's web marketing expertise and, fortunately, her life coach tag has long gone.

Karen now specialises in mentoring, teaching & training coaches, consultants and service based business owners. She can show you how to create a business model that productises and packages your offerings to make it easier for clients to buy your services.

You will find out how to automate your marketing without becoming robotic and impersonal and how to use the right marketing tools, such as blogs, email newsletters, autoresponders, Twitter, Facebook, LinkedIn and YouTube, so that you can work less whilst still increasing your revenue potential.

For more information about Karen's business mentoring, social media training programmes and Web Tech Marketing Club,
visit www.CanDoCanBe.com and subscribe to her newsletter

Follow on Twitter www.Twitter.com/CanDoCanBe

Find on Facebook www.Facebook.com/ webtechclub

Email at Karen@CanDoCanBe.com

# RESOURCES

Throughout this book I have made numerous references to dozens of tech tools and it is important that you find the right ones for you to use in your business. After all, what works for one person, may not be as easy to work for the next.

However, searching Google and researching all these tech tools can create a dangerous time suck; your magpie eye glints as it sees all these shiny shiny toys.

To help speed up your decision making process and get you taking action – rather than more web searching endlessly for weeks and weeks – I have created a list of recommended resources for you.

As you can imagine, the problem with a book such as this, is what is current today can be out of date in a matter of months. And this is especially true with the tech tools. So rather than provide a list right here, I have created a special resources page on one of my websites, just for you.

Go to www.WebTechClub.com/shinyshinyresources and you will find the latest recommended web tech tools to look at. I have added some personal comments and suggestions and will be continually adding this list in coming months.

If you would like a PDF version of this list, you can add your name and email address and get one sent to you free of charge. Plus, by signing up for the PDF version, you will be sent updated versions of the resources page as and when new recommendations are added.

If you know of a great tech tool that is not included in my list, then do get in touch with me and tell me about it. I love to discover new and useful tech tools and websites.

www.WebTechClub.com/shinyshinyresources

# THE WEB TECH CLUB

*"The most useful and easy to understand web marketing advice for small businesses today"*

Hopefully this book has helped clarify exactly what you need to do to get your business growing in the right direction. But, for some of you, more support, advice and help is needed to get you making decisions, taking action and getting your social media marketing work for you

I have lived, breathed and sweated over setting up the right web marketing systems for the past seven years, both in my own business and helping many other small business owners do the same in theirs. I know what works; and I know what doesn't.

This is why I created The Web Tech Club in September 2010 – a monthly club for small business owners to get practical, no-nonsense advice direct from me.

- Monthly live training sessions that you join via the web

- Huge library of archived videos & audios split in to easy to access sections

- No travelling time needed or being away from your desk

- Regular phone-in clinics where you can speak to me directly and get your questions answered quickly

So if after reading this book, you feel you want a place that understands your business, you want somewhere that you get help and support in setting up these web marketing systems, as well as a place where you can learn new things, new techniques, new ideas and, if necessary get a kick up the butt, then congratulations...

The Web Tech Club could be the right place for you.

For more information and grab your special Shiny Shiny book bonus go to

www.WebTechClub.com/shinyshinybook

*"Without you, I would not have met the right person to set up my blog and I'd not know about AWeber and the wonders of autoresponders. You've helped me focus my efforts, set up my workshops and create a vision of my clients to help me best attract them. You have given me such fantastic value and without it I would not be at this stage. Thank you so much, you are brilliant and remain on my "support most wanted" list." Claire Portis, www.claireportiscoaching.com*

*"I joined the Web Tech Club in October 2011 just on the very day Karen was running a webinar on how to build and run a membership site. By January 2012, my site was live and there is simply no way I could have done it without her fabulous, no nonsense advice." Tom Evans, architect of www.recipesforfreshthinking.com*

Lightning Source UK Ltd.
Milton Keynes UK
UKOW031550260912

199694UK00011B/62/P